Looking Back

Anna Fischer

Copyright © 2013 by Anna Fischer
First Edition – May 2013

ISBN
978-1-4602-1987-4 (Hardcover)
978-1-4602-1986-7 (Paperback)
978-1-4602-1988-1 (eBook)

All rights reserved.

No part of this publication may be reproduced in any form, or by any means, electronic or mechanical, including photocopying, recording, or any information browsing, storage, or retrieval system, without permission in writing from the publisher.

Produced by:

FriesenPress
Suite 300 – 852 Fort Street
Victoria, BC, Canada V8W 1H8

www.friesenpress.com

Distributed to the trade by The Ingram Book Company

Table of Contents

Acknowledgements v

Fleeing Russia vi
    March 17, 1944 vi

Introduction 1

Russia, the so-called Motherland 3
    A scene of horror by Kirichenko: 17

The Big Excitement 36

The Crippling Shock 40

Devastating News 55

The Overwhelming News 61

The Heartbreaking Search 64
    In The Book
    "KrushevRemembers" It Is Written.... 66

The Search Is Over 70

Brotherly Love 122

Death of a Husband and Father 136

Going, Going, Sold 149

A Time For Healing 168

Re-United 173
    "The Stalingrad's Front" 207
    Dear Ancestors 210

Acknowledgements

A heartfelt thanks to my loving daughters Audrey and Melinda. Without their help, I could not have even considered to write this book. As well as to my son Dale for his continued encouragement.

Fleeing Russia

March 17, 1944

Out of Russia fled we Germans
With a heavy, broken heart.
It was not a bed of roses,
Everyone to be on guard
By the door stood horse and wagon
Readied for the distant land.
Oh how we will miss our home place
That we built with our own hands
One last look – the rooms are silent
No more laughter – no more song
I can hear them whisper softly
It will never be the same without you
We have sheltered you so long.

Submitted by my sister Hilda Mueller (nee Roth)

Introduction

A revision and continuation of my first book, "Cry Out of Russia".

This autobiography unfolds the horrifying experiences of thousands of human beings, Including my parents, grandparents and relatives. You will hear of the brutal dictatorship of Stalin Communist regime, and the suffering through the deportation, murder, poverty and starvation of the German people. The stories of our forefathers go back for generations of suffering and misery.

The writing in this book tells of my unexpected experiences and undeserved treatment that my children had to live through after the tragic death of their father.

Neither my children nor I will ever forget the shocking experiences. Still today they carry the hurt that was bestowed upon them as small children.

The death of my husband and children's father brought on heart break and separation of family ties due to the accusations and treatment we had received...trying to pull the only home we had apart!

Still after over 40 years after my husbands death...the homestead still stands proud.... memories still linger on of how a death in the family can bring on greed and hatred amongst you own.

Anna Fischer

The wording and the phrasing of the sentences may not be sophisticated or far from professional, but is spoken and written from a heart so good as I still remember them and to the best of my knowledge.

Our forefathers lived from aristocracy to communism.

Russia, the so-called Motherland

After a period of several bloody civil wars and descendent, Alexi Romanov issued at law of Imperial decrees. Which divided and froze the people into rigid classes, peasants were bound to the land to work hard labor. Town people kept to their villages or cities. The church and the nobility were declared as closed classes!

Millions of peasants were looked upon as something less than animals. Czar Peter I, also known as Peter the Great; used the peasants to build his royal castle; the window on the west. Seventeen thousand workers died in St. Petersburg on a construction site that was built on a swamp. It was said that for every stone in that building, a man paid with his life.

And it was as animals that Catherine the great made calls all over Germany to lure our forefathers to immigrate to Russia. The Czar regime was desperate for hard working people to immigrate and to develop the vast land of the Ukraine.

The promise is up for calls sounded good and promising of the free land bordering money interest-free for 10 years exempt from the military for 100 years. It didn't occur to our forefathers and by the end of the 1800's, rules promising regulations were nearing and were slowly fading away.

Our great and great grand parents had to serve in the Czarist army. My grandfather and father were also called to serve his time in the Czarist army. My father served his time as a border guard in Turkmanian border. If only our grandparents knew what they were facing in their future with their families. By the last decade of the 1900th century, the time for reform had all passed in Russia. The liberated peasants were still held in bondage, in debt to the landlords. The poor continued to freeze and suffered severe beatings for any protests because of the poor living conditions. The poor had to wear sandals made from the tree barks and to live in mud huts on the edge of the splendid estate of the aristocracy.

The age old untold misery of their existence had gone on too long during the 17 to 18 hundredths. Our ancestors had immigrated to Russia in the beginning of the 1700's had a better start with all benefits. Russia was in need of trades people to run small businesses like blacksmiths and carpenters. Some with a better education such as managers were promised free land. Purchasing land was easier by the time our grandparents immigrated to Russia in the middle of the 1800's. By then the early settlers were very well established and had been, or become landlords.

The later settlers had a hard time to start, almost empty-handed. The free land, which was not so free anymore. Many of our settlers started as smaller farmers with several heads of cows and one or two teams of horses to develop the steppe. Our ancestors were looking toward owning property for their living quarters, barns and gardens. Our grandparents were living a very isolated life. No clue as to what was going on in their new surroundings. They were depending on correspondence by mail.

Looking Back

Our grand parents were aiming to get ahead and buy more land in the future, but the sale of land was almost frozen.

Had our ancestors known or could have realized as to what kind of a deadly trap they had been let to buy into. Unstable promises were offered from the Russian Imperial's throne.

Our forefathers as German settlers to their birthplace in Germany kings and rich landlords owned most the land in Germany. Most of the population reported having nothing to call their own. They never could visualize building a future for their families. They had to work in slavery for the rich landlords with very little pay.

There were many poor people looking for work struggling with hunger fighting for their daily survival it seemed the world was driven on hunger.

For our ancestors, the lure from the Russian Empire sounded promising. The imperialism pointed fingers to the under developed Steppe. To settle our forefathers to work and labor to bring it to a productive land many of our immigrants were in line with the Russians were working class working for the richer for a piece of bread for their families.

The Russian wealth was in agriculture. But our hard working immigrants brought Ukraine to a developed land. The land was all Crown land. The Czar had his grip tightened over his empire not even an inch land he parted for the millions of poor peasants. Russia of all Russia was his private estate and he was determined to keep it just the way!

Even before the 1917's our grandparents were struggling for survival through an unstable and corrupt government. Our parents knew the fighting that went on as the Reds were fighting the White. The fighting went on not for the sake of the poor people, but for the almighty power.

The ongoing struggles, through misery plus the age-old deprivation and threats were the last straw. It started with the food supplies were cut of from the big cities. Big hungers are amongst people, which started the unrest amongst the human race.

It is written in the book, the Soviets by Robert Goldstone, in January of 1905 St. Petersburg metalworkers led by a fierce priest named father capon they went on a four-day strike when this produced no effort. The workers and their wives with families determined to demonstrate in front of the royal palace.

Father Gapon wrote to the Czar. Don't believe the ministers they are cheating thee in regard to the real state of affairs: the people believe in the period they have made up their minds to gather at the Winter Palace tomorrow at 2 p.m. to lay their needs before the begging for bread. Do not fear of anything Czar Nicholas. His response was to please St. Petersburg with his family for the Palace of Tsarsko solo behind him he left a committee of police and Cossacks.

On January 22, 1905, more than 200,000 workers and their families led by Father Gapon made their way in dignified procession singing religious songs and carrying icons to the Winter Palace. They also had with them a petition requesting an eight-hour day of work and put them on a minimum wage of 50 kopek for their daily hard work.

At point-blank distance of 15 yards the police and Cossacks opened fire into the dense masses of men, women and children. They kept firing until the snow was red with blood. 500 people were massacred and thousands wounded. Father Gapon was saved but was forced to flee and found safety in Finland.

Then Father Gapon wrote to the Czar, "The innocent blood of workers their wives and children lay forever between "Thee Oh Soul Destroyer and the Russian people". Nicholas II was responsible as many man for this disaster, he not only helped ignite the bloodiest war in human history, but also left a trail of gunpowder, which blew himself his throne and the entire ancient aristocracy of Russia, sky high.

Looking Back

Anti-Bolshevik resistance shot and bayonets the entire royal family on July 16, 1918. They were held in the town of Ekaterinburg.

Lenin's government later executed the murderers. Russia found itself in a bad situation. There were civil wars on a dozen front, people were fighting for their freedom and the survival from hunger.

By 1920-1923 and onward, Russia was in the grip of a desperate famine. American food relief administration could alleviate but could not solve the problem. Furthermore industries were all dead and the current so valueless. It required 100 Ruble to purchase a loaf of bread in the big city of Moscow.

After the 1917 revolution, Russia found itself in a very unstable and grueling situation. The fighting had turned to looting, destroying shops and what ever came in their way it seemed everything crumbled and fell apart. The fighting kept on, never stopping with the Bolsheviks trying to rule the country. The same Stalin aim for communism with the grip for power.

In 1918 Fanya Kaplan attempted to kill Lenin, the leader of the Bolshevik and is succeeded by lodging a bullet in his neck. Lenin partially recovered. In May 1922 Lenin suffered a stroke, which was followed by another in December 1922. His third stroke happened March of 1923. On January 21, 1924, he suffered his final and fatal stroke.

Even before Lenin's death, the struggle for Stalin's power was steering the country toward communism. Lenin had appointed Stalin and his commissioner of nationality in the government.

In 1922 he won the post of general secretary of the Communist Party-Dzhugashvill, now conspiratorial name, "Stalin made of steel".

Stalin forced Collectivization and his five-year plan. Poverty started before the 1920s the peasants and the city people were starving. I clearly remember my father telling us of the unforgettable time in their lives and the terrible time our people had to suffer through in misery. It was the year my grandfather Wilhelm Roth was starving in 1922 in the village of Johannestal, Ukraine. Our father was telling us his father was dying of hunger. Grandfather's last dying words were, "Ich habe so hunger (I am so hungry)", while my father and brothers went door to door begging for food and as usual returning home empty-handed. It seemed at the time was rotating for misery to misery.

Everybody was living in poverty and starvation. I was born in 1926 in a time of misery and suffering from my personal experiences, as barely 4 or five years old we children had to learn fast how to go from door to door with stretched out hands begging for something to eat swollen from hunger striving for our survival. By that we have learned quickly of the forbidden rules.

In a very young each had to steal from the collective when you are hungry, you take anything you can get your hands on each. It reminded me now of wolves going hunting for their prey for us it was for our own survival. In my memories we were living in constant hunger and fear.

In the year 1928 Collectivization had begun under the banner of a crusade against the so-called Gulag's the word Gulag means power of the richer. Peasants as Gulag, overnight found them stripped of everything. Stripped of their land, homes and livestock and often of their liberty. Thousands were shipped to hard labor camps. Our grandfathers and fathers were faced with the choices of either voluntarily entering collective farms or being classified as a Gulag. Slowly unwillingly and patiently standing in line to sign up as a collective farm worker the early settlers over the years had become very wealthy. They were the owners of many hectares of land with large herds of cattle and other livestock and flourmills.

The peasants didn't like to give up what they have built up for many years. They struck back to the only way they knew how. Rather than turn over their tools houses and livestock to the government. Some of the richer villages took it into their own hands and decided to destroy everything themselves. Crops were burning in the fields, more than 17,000 horses were killed, 30,000 head of cattle and nearly 100,000 sheep. The entire German villages were declared as a disaster. And were subjected by pitched battles by the red Army units.

These naturally produced famine, now since the peasants who were resisting the government the authorities sought to get that this time that the peasants let starve. Starvation became an effective weapon against the peasants. It became so effective that the estimate of our German peasants dead, the estimate brought on by famine executions and deportations from 1928 to 1933 ranged from eight to 10 million.

In the end of course the state had won. The peasants patiently went to the collective farms as farm laborers. The people were organized and divided brihada to mow reap so and harvest people were starving and the grain was shipped and sold abroad by the Soviets regime to fill Stalin's five-year plan.

Had our forefathers known what their lives had in stake for them? What had been before them in their future by the little word immigrating to the so-called Motherland Russia? Was it to build a better future in their lives by the promises that had lured our fathers into a state of misery?

Then into misery I remember that time very well and this memory will stay with me as long as I will live. I remember clearly in my younger age five to six years my mother one day full of excitement came down from our attic had with her fabricated trap and had caught three sparrows. Mother was surprised it had worked. Mother plucking the little feathers preparing them to make supper. We had picked leaves for our soup. Patiently waiting to eat sitting on our stone fence waiting for my father to come home hoping to being something home to eat my father was working in the collective brihada feeding and preparing the horses for work early as usual to be out on the field's father always had his pants tightened up in the bottom with strings to hide and bring something home for us to eat. Stealing away the horse's feed was for our survival only today it is reminded me hungry wolves going for their prey for us it was for our survival.

I remember sitting on our stone fence waiting for some supper. Mother was preparing and cooking, suddenly, I saw Aunt Bertha's two small children coming right to our door asking my mother for something to eat asking, "Aunt Otaria, we are so hungry and our mother was gone to the neighboring village hoping to bring something home to eat". Aunt Bertha had given her two older children away to people in bigger cities of Odessa Nikolayev to save their lives from the starvation.

My mother told the children to go home and bring their own bowl and spoon so they could have a bowl of the soup. We didn't have enough dishes. My brother and I we had to share and eat together out of one dish. Mother brought out some of the soup we all got some to eat when you eat out of one dish with your sibling one learned to eat fast to get your own share. After Little Olga who was five years old and little Albert 4, had eaten their soup they got up. Little Olga holding Albert's hand walking down which was only a few houses from us. I remember my mother saying hoping that Aunt Bertha would be back soon to see her two little children still alive. The children had no more control of their own body and badly swollen from hunger.

A few days later it was noticed the two little children were not noticed on the street. My uncle Heinrich Diede was ordered to dig graves at the cemetery with another man. When they searched Aunt Bertha's house they had found the two little ones dead in their beds. They wrap the little bodies in a blanket and placed them in Aunt Bertha's baking trough and carried them to the cemetery for burial.

A few days later Aunt Bertha was found on her way home to our village. She was unconscious in a ditch beside the road still with her bag of gatherings. Aunt Bertha was brought in to relatives to regain her strength the first thing and Bertha asked was to see her two little children.

The heartbreaking news was brought to Aunt Bertha about her two little ones. They were in God's hands and resting in peace. They had been buried in the ground. Aunt Bertha sat and cried. Aunt Bertha came from a wealthy family and married into the Shorzmann family.

Shorzmann family raised my mother as an orphaned child. Grandma and grandpa Shorzmann were my mother's parents. My mother never knew of any other as her mother and father. At the age of three to four she was a great help to grandma Shorzmann. Grandma's hands were badly crippled up with arthritis. My mother grew up in the Shorzmann household and in 1925 my mother and father got married. My mother had reached the age of twenty-one years old. Grandma Shorzmann didn't like to see my mother to leave the Shorzmann house. Grandma Shorzmann was forced later on to give her son Emanuel permission to get married to Otilia Zimmerman. Otilia was a poor girl coming from a large poor family. Some of the early settlers were still in mind is that they expected to bring with them some inheritance with marriage. There was hardly any in inheritance left work to be expected.

A few years later, Otilia was saying she had brought her share of inheritance to the Shorzmann along with her a beautiful little girl Amalia, a little grand daughter. And grandma Shorzmann never favored Otilia because she came from a poor family and had no inheritance to bring with into the Shorzmann family. Grandma had not much sympathy. Amalie and I were the same age, and starting school together. We were the best of friends and the best school pals.

During my school days I spent many hours at Amalia's place, as I had called it. Aunt Otilia was trying to teach us girls how to crochet and embroider. If we were short of things and Otilia was a great help. She always found ways to help and guide us in our work and I liked Amalia's mother very much. She was helping and was a good provider. Otilia was telling that my own mother had on hard time, from early morning until dark nothing but work from little on. The family never had sent my mother to school because grandma Shorzmann needed her every minute around her to help.

My mother was illiterate. She couldn't even sign her name. This was one of the most embarrassing things for her in later years. As her children grew up and with the help from her own children mother had managed to learn to sign her name "O Roth". It didn't bother us, she was still our mother and the best and only one ever had.

As time rapidly changed the whole human race so it seemed was changing for the worse. The only store we had in the village became more and more empty and we had no money to buy anything. If material was brought in the people stood in line all night hoping to be able to purchase a few yards of fabric.

Many times as we were able to enter the store the call came, sold out. Now nothing was left but we returned home and hope for the next time we all started to get overpowered by poverty. Hunger was setting in amongst the people, and slowly the starvation, and our grain was in full force shipping and sold abroad by the Soviets nightly with the dreaded knocks on our doors.

Grandfathers, husbands, fathers and brothers were led away as enemies to the country or to the people, and the state, we never knew who would be next, the most heartbreaking to see our loved ones be led away, the steady harassing of our people in the middle of the night never ended. Everything was silenced by the fear of more deportations.

In the morning like nothing had or was happening during the night the family went on with their work with silence, not a word was spoken. You could see the children walking forlorn and sad faced, amongst the relatives, neighbors and amongst their school friends. Coming to our classes we children as young we were we could see sometimes a child standing in a corner crying you didn't need to ask why.

Our school years were the years of poverty. It all depended on our harvested crop. If the year was promising and our norm was delivered to the state, the pressure on us was not as intense. We were always hoping to be able to fill the five-year plan. The rest of the state was not concerned how we people survived struggling in poverty and hunger.

In my younger years speaking of education, it was almost impossible to attend schools regularly. When we were suffering from hunger our minds were not on learning only on food and also in the winter we had no warm clothing to wear. I remember times when my mother gave me her shawl to wrap around me to go to school and some time no shoes to wear. We had our feet wrapped in rags. My Uncle Heinrich was a shoemaker by trade. He would sew us boots from rags but when the weather was wet and rainy we had to stay home. Our school days were very irregular. I early spring, as it had warmed up, us children went barefoot to school. If we had nothing to eat we stayed home as well. Some of the children didn't pass onto the next grade and one was lucky to be able to reach grade 8.

Overnight our German schoolteacher had disappeared and was replaced with a teacher who spoke nothing but Russian. We were confused and disappointed when we learned in the morning that we were faced with the Russian teacher. We didn't understand or speak the Russian language.

The only language we knew was out our mother tongue of German, which we were now deprived and was forbidden to speak in the classes also on the premises of the schoolyard. By back the children started to Stand in hidden corners where they could whisper. You could see the schoolyard were empty the children stopped playing games. As the authority saw not our schools have not progressed, then they decided and forced the children from the neighboring Russian small village Gubracy to walk every morning 3 km to our village of Johannestal in hopes that the children would mingle with each other hand adapt faster to the Russian language. It was difficult to adapt to the new schooling and language and this hindered our progress in school, and many times were held back. We were failing in our grades. The attendance at school stayed the same. It changed every year if we had a little more to eat then again nothing to wear. We were all stricken with poverty looking for word to reach the end of the school year.

Then you were right away enrolled to the labor force as a collective laborer. We all had our norm to fill a collective. The only good thing nobody was around our work to stop us from speaking our own language. The only system the Russians were able to install in us German people was the fear and being very cautious of everything to look around you before you speak. One little wrong word you could end up being led away and we would never know what went on around us, everything was kept a secret; we only knew and were sure of when we were hungry. We wanted to eat and nothing was available. The saddest was seeing a child crying for hunger, and not being able to ask for food, was too young to understand why there was no food to eat. There was nothing to offer. It was in time looking back the tremendous amount of hope from year to year that had built up on the German population always saying may be next year, maybe-maybe!

In mean time we suffered in poverty and hunger struggling for our survival.

In the early 30s in the Ukraine as I remember was the worst and biggest hunger and poverty in human history. Collectivization from 1928 to 1933 was the biggest terror to the countryside. Nobody knew or ever will know how many millions of our people have perished through torture and deportation. Collectivization had brought us nothing but misery and brutality. Millions of our people, grandparents and fathers were

Looking Back

led away from their families as enemies to the people and the state they had to go through harsh interrogations for hours with severe kicking, punching, squeezing their fingers between door jams forced to confess of things they were not guilty of.

Through torture they were forced to confess what the regime wanted to know: confessing of being a spy for the Western country and confessing of being a Gulag at times even forced to sign their own confessions.

It is written in the book Khrushchev remembers as the following story: By two members of the political Bureau conversations in the city of Kiev with Towarish Demchenko who was the first Secretary of Kiev's Regional and Anastas Ivanovich Mikoyan. Demchenko said, "Anastas Ivanovich, does comrade Stalin for that matte, or does anyone in the political Bureau know what is happening in the Ukraine"? "Well if not: I'll give you some idea. A train recently pulled into Kiev loaded with corpses who had people that had starved to death. It had picked up corpses all the way from Buldovia to Kiev. I think someone or somebody better inform Stalin about this situation".

You could see how abnormal the state of affairs had developed in the party. Afraid of approaching Stalin, it had meant that it could be the end of your own life, and sometimes the whole family would disappear overnight, never to be accounted for or heard of.

I remember at harvest time after the fields were harvested and quoted as finished, we went out on the harvested fields looking for some heads of wheat that had broken off and was left behind on the ground. After walking all day on the stubble searching and picking up the heads of grain to clean and cook for our meals. Sometimes the authorities came out investigated our picking wheat. If it happened that you had in your bag a nice little pail of heads of wheat, it was taken away.

If that was repeated a couple of times they would call a meeting amongst our people that harvested. Accusing them saying they deliberately left the heads of wheat on the ground, which was needed to fill the five-year plan. Our people were accused of picking up kernels from the ground as a crime and were punished.

If we children were successful in bringing some heads of grain home, we cleaned the wheat kernels out of the heads, and mother was able to cook the wheat for our meal to eat. But that was not without a price to pay for some of our people. You were forced to do everything in secrecy, and caused the whole country in the Ukraine to live in silence.

The begging of children going door to door never really stopped. There came also children from the neighboring villages knocking on our doors, rarely asked for a piece of bread because they knew we never had bread for a long time. They were asking for mamalika, potatoes or maybe a handful of grits. We were cooking our "gasche", meaning heavy porridge, everything was appreciated, even potato peelings. It was a sad sight to see and worse to live under. It is hard to understand if you have never experienced living that kind of life in poverty and hunger.

The people had prepared a petition for ration cards for the Ukrainian people. Khrushchev went to see Stalin at his Sochi. Khrushchev was accused of requesting an outrageous amount of ration cards to feed the people. Khrushchev could not express how murderous the telegram depressed him. Khrushchev saw clearly now the whole tragedy, which was not only hanging over Khrushchev personally but over the whole Ukrainian people. Famine was now inevitable.

Stalin's response -- our last hope that could have been prevented. Khrushchev as a member of the committee was in fear of his own life. In a blink of an eye you could be thrown into the lubyanka, the secret police, and in prison in the heart of Moscow. Now it was predicted famine was strong under way, soon Khrushchev's was receiving letters and reports from collective farm workers and from their chairman. This was the heart breaking letters, the chairman from the collective farm wrote," Well Comrade Khrushchev, we have delivered our quota to the state, but we have given everything away nothing is left for us, we are sure the state and the party won't forget us. Khrushchev said that since I was the head of the state and the party that people were depending on me for help again Stalin flatly turned down Khrushchev's request for help. Kirichenko, who also was a member of the committee, was sent to investigate the collective farms to check on how people were surviving the winter. He was told to go see a woman who worked there.

And here is how Kirichenko described it:

A scene of horror by Kirichenko:

I found a scene of horror. "By entering the woman's home I was in shock", Kirichenko said. "The woman had the corpse of her own child on the table and was cutting it up. She was chattering away as she was working and said, "we'd already eaten Manuchka (little Maria). Now we will salt down Vanushka (little Ivan). This will keep us for some time". Can you imagine the woman had gone crazy with hunger and was butchering her own children?

Kirichenko minds going back to the time of misery but there was nothing they could do. The report to Stalin it only fumed his anger all the more accusing Khrushchev of being soft and saying, "they are deceiving you and trying to pull your reserves".

Khrushchev as leader of the original committee was flatly denied help for the people. Hoping the people who are reading my book get the understanding the desperate suffering our forefathers had to endure. When Khrushchev as the leader of the original committee and later became the leader of Russia after Stalin died in 1953.

Khrushchev acknowledges and tells of his memories of the happenings in the Ukraine. Khrushchev tells the tragedy of the famine years in Ukraine in the book "Khrushchev remembers".

Even as my own memories of the famine years in the Ukraine, as the German settlements were forced into collective farm labor, the experiences of deportation of our own people in the middle of the night. Some in the winter in deep snow and some of our families who know and have the feeling being on the list to be deported to Siberia, Archangels or some to Ural Mountains, to the most coldest northern parts. Some family's fathers and mothers packed up their children and escaped on foot in the middle of the night walking into different villages hiding out avoiding to be recognized and to protect their identity. They stayed in the different places and lived in constant fear with their families.

Moving from village to village, many times hiding under a different name for years. Just a few of them to mention for our village Johannestal were the August Shorzmann family, the Schempp family, the Schmidt family, the Hienle family, the Diede family and the Delzer family were hiding, and on the move for years to save their lives.

The families simply packed and bundled up the children, and their little bundles on their backs, disappearing into the unknown. Some were hiding with their relatives for a short time to avoid to be recognized. Some families were saved from deportation by confessing to crimes that had hurt others.

I met Jacob Diede and his wife Caroline living in deadwood USA. Jacob and Caroline are from our village of Johannestal. Jacob was telling my brother Adolf during our visit to deadwood USA that Jacob's family, at the time of his young age, his parents from 1922-1938 the family was chased five times out on the street. There was nowhere to go when you were branded as a "Gulag". You were staying as their Gulag. Jacob's father was deported and executed never to come back and his mother starved.

Looking Back

By the German invasion of the Ukraine in 1941 some of our people in secret hiding were returning home and some of our villagers in hiding never were coming home to claim their homes and land. By a rare coincidence our family was reunited with Andrea's Seiler family and the Schempp family in Canada. Both families were from our village of the Johannestal. The Schempp family was on of many families never returned by the Hitler invasion.

Mr. Schempp was explaining during the conversation with my father, that they were hiding out in many different places and were patiently waiting. What time will bring us to Schempp was saying the main reason by not returning home was the struggle of uncertainty and fear of the time in the past. Mr. Schempp was saying, "If I had returned to my home to file my claim I would not be any farther than I am today, might be even worse". Father and Mr. Schempp were admitting that they were the lucky and fortunate ones to be able to immigrate to Canada to a country they can feel free from their horrifying past. The silence to fear that Stalin had inflicted is deep rooted in us people.

Some of that fear will stay till we take it with us in our graves. Many of our homes and our old country were ruined under the communist rule. Some of our bigger homes were used to store grain and some homes the collective people had to build long rows of barns to house milking cows, some horse barns at the brihada large pig barns also for the big herds of sheep. Our once nice clean village was ruined. We were deprived of so much; therefore we had lost our pride. We didn't have anything to be proud of, all was left our daily routine work.

As a young child I had witnessed some of our people were chased out of their home place. Moving in to empty home where the people were deported or had starved by working in the collective. Sometimes the people had to take part to rip down their own homes built a hog barn. Our church was used for different things. Some years it was used as a storage facility. The church building didn't resemble as our church as it once stood. The steeple had been removed, and now resembled yet just another building. Therefore our families and forefathers had no place for prayer in God's House. The metal and iron crosses from the church and cemetery was dismantled. It was told that there was a greater need and purpose for the iron and metal to build ammunition to protect our country, this was Stalin's philosophy.

I remember we were celebrating the New Year. As children all had been invited to the church building. The children were receiving their report cards. The children with the highest marks out of the classroom received a gift. We were given gifts of remnant fabric to make clothing. My brother Gottlieb received a gift two years in a row. There was enough material for one pair of pants and a shirt. Mother was very proud of him.

Our mother was occupied in so many different jobs milking cows feeding pigs, and tending to so many things like cleaning barns early in the morning before going out to the fields. The men's jobs were with the horses, tilling and seeding the massive hectares of land that bordered on to the neighboring village. Later in spring my mother and the younger girls went out to the field to weed and hoe to keep the crops clean. Each woman and girl had a norm to fill. In our collective we had planted corn, beats, potatoes and sunflowers. There was always plenty to do from early morning to evening. In the summertime every morning a barrel of water was supplied for us to drink.

That was where I came in to fill my responsibilities by taking care of my younger siblings. At the age of eight years old I had to milk our one cow. Each family was allowed to own one cow. Each family had their quota of butter fat to fill and delivered to the state. Every milking time the milk had to be taken to the collective milk separator to remove the butterfat. I always needed help to lift the pail of milk into the separator, as I was too short. After the milk was separated, I ran home and gave the skim milk to my siblings. By 11 o'clock I went to the kindergarten class and each of us children received a ladle full of soup. I ran home and gave my brother some of that soup. My brother Gottlieb's responsibility was to rock the cradle when the baby was crying until I got back with the soup. We each had some soup. I made sure there was some left for my mom. I took the baby and the soup with my brother Gottlieb and walked out in the field where my mother was working. Mother would nurse the baby and at the same time would eat her soup. There was no food to take to my mother. In my younger years I grew up with big responsibilities. As young as I was, I knew if mother had no soup or anything else to eat she would not be able to nurse the baby.

I considered myself as a child with grown-up responsibilities. Many times I let my emotions take over and went and hid and cried. I wanted to play with the other girls who were more fortunate enough to have more time and able to go splashing in the water by our dam. But in my case we had younger children, then myself to look after. As I was the oldest in the family I always had received more punishment when work was not done at home. In the terrible heat I carried the baby home and by then I was exhausted. I told my brother to lie down to rest with the baby in its crib. After they had fallen asleep, I also laid down for a rest. I was very tired.... every day the same routine. I went through my own time of suffering, never complaining. We knew this was our life with no other way out. Even with the years changing. Some years our hopes were high by receiving a little more wheat and corn the next year began the suffering of hunger because the government demanded to return a portion of our supply after the collective toward the five-year plan that was not filled; the shocking fear that was hanging over us. Some people tried to hide a little bit of wheat that they had. The government warned if not giving up the wheat freely, they came by force, from house to house. If you had something hid, and it was found, you can be sure your father would be deported as a traitor to the country or as a Gulag. To be deported to slave labor camps in Siberia or Archangels to the coldest northern part. I remember I was about seven years old. We recognized the wagon going from house to house. With a long iron stick with a magnet tip, the stick was poked into the walls. If something was hidden and was found, your loved ones were taken away. As I saw the wagon driven by the informers and the secret police came close to our home only three houses away. I ran into our kitchen, mother and father were discussing something. I called out, "Mom the wagon is coming". I overheard my father saying, "If they find it, I will be gone". I never knew that my parents were hiding grain. Just at that moment my mother said, "Carl as God's will". Mother walked over and reached under a little stool and took out a hatchet. I stood back and watched. Mother grasped the hatchet in her hands and I began to panic.

 I was afraid of what might happen next. I always focused towards our door to escape in case something going wrong. I saw mother standing with a hatchet in her hand. It looked scary. Then my mother went toward our kitchen window started to aim against the lower window. I stood watching in fear. I didn't know if mother had gone mad. Then with several blows the wheat came out from inside the wall, and ran down on the floor making a puddle. My father took a breath. He seemed a little more relaxed now.

 Without any warning our door flung open. There stood Jelka Chernetzky and Wanja Kolomenchuk. Immediately before any word was spoken my mother approached Jelka saying, "We had grain hidden and this is all we have and we're willing to give it up freely". The two informers were sweeping up the grain. My mother stood begging with a small bowl in her hand saying to Jelka, "Please leave us a little bowl full of wheat for my children. We are hungry". Jelka said, "It cannot be done, we have to take everything". Before the two left our house they made my father sign that the grain was given freely and willingly. My mother started crying, and I couldn't help my tears were also flowing down my cheeks. My mother had said to my dad, "Karl, as God's will, but at least you are still with us".

Within next few days, I sat on the stone fence, and noticed that most feared wagon was coming toward my Aunt Rose's house. I ran fast to tell my Aunt Rosa that I saw the wagon coming. They stopped right in front of her house. Without warning they entered her house.

They demanded they get ready. The family was to be deported. Aunt Rosa started to cry while gathering her two children and getting them ready. With only a little bundle for each they were led away to the Brihada, which is a building to wait for their father to follow. Their father, my Uncle Heinrich was lying sick in bed. He was suffering from some type of lung disease and was confined to bed. They demanded that my Uncle Heinrich get up of his bed several times. They demanded that he follow his family who were waiting for him beside the stone fence. They were not even allowed to go inside the barn, and it was already late in the fall and the nights were getting cool. Aunt Rosa and her two children had to stand there for a very long time and were getting very tired. Back in their home they were still trying to get Uncle Heinrich to get out of his bed. They would stomp their boots on the floor demanding for him to get up, and out of bed. But they would have never ventured close to the bed, for they feared that whatever he had was contagious. They would keep on badgering Uncle Heinrich over and over again.

Uncle Heinrich was not going to do what they wanted. Whatever they wanted, he was not willing to leave his home. He told them that he was very sick and running a high fever and if he were to get out of his bed, he would die. "I wish to die in my own bed", he said. They started to move away knowing they couldn't win. This was a rare instance that had worked. Aunt Rosa with her crying children was allowed to return to their home. All the little clothing that they had then was gone from her home. Rose stood crying, father went home took brought

Anna Fischer

a blanket from our bed and brought it to Aunt Rose to cover the children during the night. Rose was saying that she had the feeling that this would hit her family. Rosa had asked my mother for help sewing rags together for mittens and wrap around on boots for the children two weeks before.

It was hard to witness what went on around us. We as children never to my memory had a happy lifestyle anything to be excited about. We went on day to day. We only knew the poverty and hunger. Brother Adolf was born in 1934 when I was eight years old. My sister Hilda was born in the year 1937. It was very hard on me now we were four children in the family. After my baby sister was born mother was allowed to stay home to take care of the baby. Because my mother wasn't working, we received less food rations, which were so desperately needed for the family. We received for our working day grind barley for cereal to cook our porridge for breakfast.

I felt so sorry for my mother. I know she was worried dad was working alone. It wasn't enough to feed and support us all. Now we were a family of six. Mother was planning to go to work. I said to my mother that she should stay home and I would work her norm hoeing and weeding in the field. I went out to the fields working side-by-side with grown women. It was very hard.

I had to admit it felt good to receive our portion of flour to bring home. It was a good help for my mother with the younger siblings and they felt more comfortable having my mother at home. But my mother felt sorry for me. Then I stayed home and she went out to work. The hardest was for me at harvest time I could feel I was not being strong enough to do the heavy work. As soon as harvest started the grain was delivered to fill the five-year plan. Some of our grain was stored on piles on the threshing spot for later delivery.

The later harvest like corn and cotton were dumped in our homes. Corn cobs had to be husked, and cotton to be opened up with our fingers, in hopes to get the cotton out. The cobs were dumped in our room where we ate and slept. We were relieved when the many hours we spent to finish up and delivered it was hard night the crawling over the piles and the same in the morning. Our homes were not too big a main room was for sleeping eating and all the rest of work was done the kitchen by the time the heating material was stored there was only room left for mother to cook.

In 1937 to 1939 Stalin did his mobilization, all our young men and boys was said to serve in the army. Very few were in training most were sent to hard labor camps as traitors and enemies to the country or were branded as a Gulag.

We never had received any messages from them later we were hearing most of our people had been executed the rest was never allowed to get in touch with their families.

To our surprise over ten years after World War II my cousin Amalia Roth was deported from Poland to Siberia Amalia through the Red Cross had found her brother on the Asian border. He was sent there to work hard labor. That was when we were hearing the terrible things that were happening.

Cousin Daniel Roth after being reunited after many years with his sister Amalia. Many of our deportees after Stalin's death had regained some freedom and many were moving to Asia from Siberia where the weather was more humane warm or Daniel saying it was hard knowing you have left family behind.

Women and children and aged old man were left behind to do the work. A hand full of men, were left to stay behind to do the hard physical work with horses.

Luckily my father was one of them because my parents were listed as a mixed marriage. My grandmother, Marie was a widow when she became pregnant from a rich land owner. Afraid of losing her child, she befriended a homeless man by the name of Myron Belanov. They got married and when my mother was born, she took on the Belanov name. It was my mother's stepfather name that saved my father several times during his life because of my mother's adopted Russian name she went by.

In 1940 we had an agriculturalist in our home by the name Valentine Kaul he was a young German he was telling my father he comes from Semphoropol, to further his schooling he had to sign off from his parents never to come in contact with them and had to join the Comsomols organization. Mr. Kaul most had trust in my father to tell him that. Mr. Kaul put my father in charge of the wheat treatments and Kaul was testing and measuring the treatments. It just so happened that that year was a very dry spring and the crop was coming up very patchy. The collective representatives were calling for an upcoming meeting. My father became very nervous and afraid that they were going to pass on the blame on him for the failed crops. My father went and paid a visit to Semjan Barsky, he was Jewish my father explained to Semjan about the upcoming meetings and the problem with the dry patches of crops. Semjan was in charge of collecting the butterfat from the villagers.

My father told him about the upcoming meeting. Collective representatives would likely blame me for the seed treatments.

After Semjan had listened to my father, Semjan told my father Carl to leave it up to Sam. The meeting was called, Sam had appeared also with the agriculturalist, Mr. Kaul. The meeting started with fists hammering on tables. Mr. Sam Barsky got up and started to speak as well as the agriculturalist. Mr. Kaul and Sam were both speaking in favor of my father, stating that everything was done accordingly to the plan. The crops had not yielded well due to the lack of moisture it... was a very dry year. My father was relieved that he wasn't blamed for the crop failure. My father would have been taken away and have never seen his family again.

Years later I approached my father while he sat on a stool crying. This was very rare to see my father crying and show such emotion.... this is when my father broke down and proceeded to tell me this very story and how Sam Barsky and Mr. Kaul saved his life.

The same year my father was put in charge of keeping records of all the collective workers what and how much they were working daily the women weeding hoeing. It was most devastating task for him being partially illiterate barely making it to grade 3 not being able to go to school living in poverty his parents had starved. Dad was very uncomfortable. He was not able to do this kind of work but he had no choice. My cousin Rosa who was one year younger than me, my father asked us for help.

Days and evenings to no end we would rewrite dad's work. My father writing was poor especially in Russian, my dad wanted to hand in a good report according to the work what was done and every women's work after the end of the harvest time and the desired quota for the state and the five-year plan was filled and the seed cleaned and what was left was divided it showed the poor working people where the last on the list.

To our surprise, in 1940 the first time in years, we were receiving more than ever for our working days. Families were able to take a bag of wheat to the flour mill in our neighboring village Landou. And bring flour home for the first time in years mother were able to bake bread. Myself I couldn't remember when I last time was eating bread even if was whole bread heavy and dark but it tasted so good all so now my mother was able to stay home and look after her children even a baby born 1939 Katerina a baby girl there was plenty work for her with five children mother and father there were seven people in our family by now I was listed as full-time collective worker. With the age of thirteen years, I completely stayed out of school for the Russian language didn't take us far. I was working side-by-side with grown women I was determined to work what came my way or where ever they put me on to work, I was even asked to work at the Harman meaning threshing spot keeping up with adults was not always rosy for me but I had to stick to my work. Some days I was put on the dirtiest job behind the threshing machine to remove the straw.

Some other time I was put on turning the wheat-cleaning machine it was hard work some types of seed was cleaned and stored for the next years seeding time.

Summer was very hot, and we were searching for a shady spot to eat our lunch. I had settled under our water wagon that held our drinking water in a wooden barrel. That day my mother was able to put a hard-boiled egg in my lunch bag with bread and a clove of garlic. Everybody started to eat. I rubbing my bread crust with the garlic looking forward to eating my egg last.

Uncle Heinrich my father's youngest brother said to me, "Anna, give me your egg if you don't want to eat it, I will eat it". At that moment I felt so sorry for him. I gave my egg to Uncle Heinrich. Uncle Heinrich had a large family to provide for and was working alone.

His first wife Anna Auch had passed away. Sickness struck. Typhus spread quickly. Anna died leaving behind for children and her youngest baby boy was six months old the same age as my brother Adolf. My mother had to nurse or breast-feed two babies. Uncle Heinrich's wife and was eager to help support the family. Anna went early in the morning before daylight with a pale to her father's barn and was milking their cow. Running home now she had more milk for her children as usual and the stepmother Caroline went to milk their cow in the morning. Caroline said to her husband, "Johan better feed the cow, she hardly gives me milk". She never suspected that somebody was milking her cow. Anna kept that up until she became sick and died. Uncle Heinrich had no other choice but to find somebody in a hurry to look after his four children. He married a middle-aged woman by the name of Hulda Roth from our village Johannestal also was a distant relative of Heinrich. There were still three sisters; their father Michael Roth was deported as a Gulag, their mother had starved. Their only brother Emil was also deported as a Gulag. Leaving behind two children, Amalie and Johan the sisters of Emil took care of the two children I went to school with Johan he was my age and all the women had stayed in their original home place.

They were by then middle-aged women, 30 and beyond. For years Hulda neglected the four children from Uncle Heinrich's first marriage. Forever she was visiting with her sisters, they were inseparable. Uncle Heinrich was very stressed; working hard at the collective and the constant worries about his four children, many times home alone. I remember my father was telling my mother that his brother Heinrich was saying if it doesn't get better he feels forced to send Hulda back to her sisters. My aunt Rosa was very concerned and said to her brother Heinrich to calm down, maybe in a while it will get better. Maybe Hulda will realize in time that she has now a responsibility to do what a mother has to do with children. It was to understand Hulda's family was branded as Gulag, their father deported and executed and their mother had starved. The sisters were left alone. Their brother was also deported and they were raising his two children.

The sisters grew very close. They continued to stay tight knit even after she was brought into my Uncle Henry's home to care for the children. One day Rosa said to my mother, "how about taking the girls over to aunt Rose's place and wash their clothing and wash their hair"? It was done also they rubbed gasoline on the hair to get the lice under control

We all had our share on the blood-sucking creatures. Maybe Hulda will realize that she has to look after the girls. Mother said that maybe Hulda will get mad. Rosa replied that she would never know; the girls have to be quiet. It got little better after while after she started to have her own children. And her other sisters got married to widower. So everybody stuck to his or her own work and for uncle Heinrich it was more of a relief because he was now content that his children were looked after. To our surprise after the harvest of 1940 we received a little more wheat and corn. We were able to trade for flour. The women were able to bake bread and we were able to have some eggs for the family to eat. The sudden changes were hard to understand after all the seeding was done. In 1941, the call came to draft all available men to the Russian Army. The whole village was in panic. We had no idea what was going on. The drafting of our older people of our fathers made us uneasy. I remember all the men had to gather at the brihada, they all were loaded on horse pulled wagons. Each of the men equipped with forks and sticks as their weapons, and headed in the eastern direction.

I remember children and mothers standing waving goodbye and crying, the families staying behind with worries.

In a short time we were waken during the nights with one heavy thundering noise at times shaking. We thought bad weather was coming our way. In the morning it appeared to be the nicest, bright and sunny day. We thought the weather had passed over us. But it was going on night after night. Our mothers starting to worry about our dad's gone. We thought maybe our father were taken to dig trenches and the nightly thundering was believed the Red Army is maneuvering by Achakov) Odessa. It was known to be as training station for the Red Army the thundering kept its nightly shaking and lightning in the sky.

Almost one good week had gone by since our father was taken away. We knew we would never hear from our father again, unless one was lucky to come home. The women were hoping that our men had shelter for the nights. They were taken in a hurry there was no time to prepare. They didn't even have blankets to cover during the night.

As the fog had thinned out in the morning, mother came rushing in the house saying that if you like to see something come quick. Mother was explaining that our neighbor Sophie

Looking Back

Will was saying, "Look really hard". Focusing to the south of our village we were standing by our fence waiting. As the fog slowly lifted we were able to see more clearly. It looked like a long train standing about three-quarter mile from our village. But people stopped to think, how could that be, we have no train tracks by our area or surroundings.

Oh somebody popping up suddenly it was again our neighbor Sophie Will, "I tell you what I think it is", and we all listened. She thought that it might be the Russian Army. They are moving toward Achakov to their maneuvering spot. We were all content with her answer, but there was no movement.

The women were starting to get more and more restless. There still was no replay and no answers from their men. The next morning during a calm quiet night, we were strongly convinced that our men were hauled away to dig safety trenches.

It was 1941 the beginning of June we were surprised by some beautiful motorbikes. On each bike sat a spotless dressed Russian uniform. Officers all decorated as higher-ranking officers. They stopped and asked in fluent Russian if we saw any Russian soldiers in our village or if we know where some were hiding. Our neighbor lady was speaking to them as she spoke the language very well.

All were feeling sorry for any escapee, as they would be immediately shot. The soldiers on their bikes left and the women returned with their worries toward their husbands and fathers. A short time passed since that ordeal, then we heard singing. Beautiful voices echoed in the village. We didn't know what to think, the voices became louder and clearer. We could understand that German words to the songs, but we didn't know what to think. Finally over the prairie to the southwest direction, a huge amount of soldiers come marching and singing. As they come closer to our village, we recognized the German songs. I remember to this day the day they came marching in nice uniforms. I remember the song Heute Gehort Uns Deutschland und Morgen Die Ganse Welt.

I was so overwhelming, for so many years we were almost afraid to speak our language, and now to hear somebody singing German out loud. I was especially fond of singing as a young girl. The leaders were driving in on open jeep. We had never seen something like a vehicle. We led such sheltered lives. It was so new to us. The jeeps and motorbikes were stopped to ask if we were Germans.

Our neighbor lady, with her loud voice screamed out, "Yes we are all Germans". The soldiers said that they came to free us from communism. You are brothers and sisters. We come to free you from the misery. The riders on the bikes asked where our men were. We see women and children. Roughly one and one half weeks ago, they were taken away. Sophie our neighbor was asked to do the speaking. Sophie was telling them that the last mobilization was down one and one half weeks ago. Mostly the older men were taking away on horse pulled wagons toward the east. The Germans assured the women to relax that your husbands were kept back by our German troops. Your men were more than likely under the German occupations hands, and would be held as prisoners of war. They assured us that it wouldn't take long until your men are able to return home. All German men will be released and returned home to their families. We felt so relieved. But so many of our loved ones that have been taken away earlier in 1937 to 1939 would never came back. Mostly were executed or starved in prison. We will never know how many millions more have perished under Stalin's rule with his criminal actions.

The villagers slowly were settling down. Minds racing as to what this all will bring us. We still were not sure of ourselves not knowing will all this be for real. Will we really have our freedom? Will what we were living through return? We didn't want to go through that life again. For now it sounded good.

Looking Back

It seemed that we had our freedom. Free to go to bed without harassment, or be let away from your family. For now we were having our freedom through the German occupation. We did not want to admit that we were still not sure of our future.

It was scary feeling being able to roam. The collective was stripped. By now the people were slowly settling down, speculating what this all was going to bring us. We are not sure of ourselves. We didn't like to think of our past. For now we were having our freedom through the German occupation that had freed us. The collective was stripped of all the animals. Horses, cows, sheep and pigs were divided amongst the people in the village. Some homes with larger capacity were able to house more of the animals every home had received what they were able to bring under and provide shelter.

My father had brought home four horses, two nice teams, three milking cows, six pigs and sheep. The only thing was now questioned was the land that had caused a concern for our people.

The only decision was to work the land together like before. Every morning my father took his two favorite teams of horses and went to work. Everything went smoothly after the seeding was done. The men were working hard to fix some of the damaged machinery that was lying on rusted up piles.

The blacksmith was working from early morning until the evening to weld the broken plows and harrows to get us ready for harvesting time. Every household had planted a large garden area to provide for the necessities for winter. Everybody had to work and help with the harvest. At threshing time I went every day to work so mother could stay at home with the younger children. In 1942 my sister Rosa was born with a new baby, mother was happy to stay home to do the chores. After the harvest we had received a nice supply of wheat, which was stored in our attic. Also sun seeds for our oil that was stored from the years before. Everything was divided amongst our families. After so many years the women were able to bring bread on the table for the families.

Mother now was able to bake bread kuchen, also the nice fried potatoes. They tasted so good. Everything was so tasteful to eat after suffering starvation for so many years. Now the men were loading bags of wheat to take to the flourmill in the village of Landau, which was only 10 km from our village of Johannestahl. Now finally for years the women were able to bring bread on the table for their families. The time had come what our people were longing for, for so many years. We had now our own butter cheese for the winter. We also had our pork meet our sausage not to forget our eggs. We were satisfied food was playing the biggest role in our life.

At the time of our occupation by the Germans, we prepared for harvest. Everyone was out in full force. No more knocking on our doors in the middle of the night. We were sure that the informers wouldn't bother us anymore. Deep in our conscience we were not completely sure because everything seemed too quiet. We were for too many years living under terror.

I couldn't believe I saw Jelka Chernetzky walking with a kerchief on her head and pitchfork over her shoulder. She was coming to help the rest of the workers. Everybody was sort of shocked. We never ever saw Jelka working.

In a short while an open jeep arrived with the German officer and his fraulein came to pick up Jelka. Jelka seated in the back, the German officer headed the jeep toward the calcimine pit.

Right after the German occupation changes took place. It was not for us to know. We were more concerned for now that we had food. Hoping in time that we were able to travel to the bigger cities and trade our food for the much needed clothing and bedding for our children and families. We knew under the German occupation the big cities were suffering from hunger. The war was still on in a very progressive stage deeper into the Russian territories. There was no time to build a government at that stage. I am certain the Ukrainian people were striving for freedom. They all were suffering poverty under Stalin's dictatorship. Stalin had the whole Russia under his thumb.

And through this whole population was silenced, it took a long time for the German people to build trust, and that it was the German people were debating and full of fear. We were still with hidden fear and mistrust. But for now we were happy.

The Big Excitement

Now our village started to show life. We were with our hard work on the land. Still working together, it would take years to for every landowner to work for their own. But there was not enough farm equipment left. Everything lay on a pile of rusted up rubbish. What was destroyed under Stalin's ruling and now for the time under the German occupation the time started to look promising. All our trade people were working almost around the clock to fix everything that still could be repaired. Wagons were repaired, our rusted up plows, seeders, and fanning mills. Everybody was on the job and was feeling content. Everything went slow and smoothly.

To our surprise, a big announcement was made that a new pastor from Germany would be visiting the German villages. We were asked to prepare for confirmation for the ages of 14 and older.

As well if people wanted to get married. The pastor would marry them in the church. There were married couples that wanted to pledge their marriage in front of the pastor and the church. Also announced was that baptisms would take place the same time. Everybody was excited. My father with several other men had decided to travel to the city's big market in Odessa.

Looking Back

Mother packed eggs and butter to send along with my father to bring material for a dress for my confirmation. My father brought home a dress that was already cut. After lying the pieces out, to our disappointment there were pieces missing. I was heartbroken that I didn't have a new dress for my confirmation. My mother was said, you know what we will do; we will go see Aunt Bertha to borrow a dress from her daughter. Once we borrowed the dress...what kind of shoes was I supposed to wear? It was summertime, we could have gone barefoot but my mother was certain that she knew someone that had a second-hand pair of shoes. Even though they were very tight I suffered for that day. At least I had a pair of shoes to wear.

On that special day, there were 300 people taking part in the festivities. Some couples also attended, but mostly younger people came for the confirmation also some couples wanted their marriage vows performed by the pastor as well as baptisms. It was a wonderful day, under the summer sky as our church had been ruined, and was too small for such a crowd. The church service was held which was a wonderful occasion for the younger children. We were full of excitement when they announced that the BDM girls from Germany would pay us a visit.

BDM stood for Pure German Girls. They were coming to introduce themselves in hopes that we join the BDM. The girls danced and sang, showing off their white blouses, black skirts and ties. They chose and nominated a BDM leader from one of our older girls for training.

We all were to sign up to belong to the BDM nice young girls. We were very vulnerable and excited of the out come; we were satisfied for the first time in my life. I saw the people smiling. It was nice to see the happiness in their faces. There was happiness for those few days. How sad it was that the missing men from the village were not able to see their children and grandchildren on this occasion. We were content; it was a big change for our people from years before. It would still take years to return to normal, if it ever would.

For the time the people were content, but deep in our hearts these was still some hesitation deeply rooted. The word freedom was what we were longing for. For us German people that time was welcomed with open arms. We were aiming for the speedy move forward deeper into Russian territory in hopes of discovering our missing people, who had disappeared or were deported earlier. There were so many of our younger man led away, never any messages or to be heard from. They were all sent to hard labor camps to build bridges and canals over swamps in Siberia. Some were taken to work deep in the coalmines. For us now, the only thing we could do was to wait and see what the future brings. For now, we had our freedom with all of us working together; building up our village after everything was destroyed through generations of Stalin's regime.

It was the beginning of 1944, after barely three years since the Germans freed us. Free from our misery and suffering. In spring, the men were getting prepared to get out to the fields to start seeding as usual. Rumors were circling around that the German Army was in trouble. Our people were not taking it seriously at all. By now our trust was built so high and strong for the German occupation. The rumors continued, it was said that the German Army was retreating and on the move toward the West. We began noticing that the German military was heading toward the West. We were overcome with worries, but our trust with the Germans was strong. The German people started questioning the rumors, but we were told not to worry. We were told to get ready and prepare for seeding. Have no fear. Everything is under control. Concern and worry began. We were simply told to continue with seeding our crops.

The frost just got out of the ground and was too wet to go out into the fields. The men were all prepared to start seeding the massive land. Seeding time started usually in the beginning of

Looking Back

March. By the end of March the seeding was done; everything went slow with the small equipment that we were left with.

We thought that if there were any changes that we would be notified, or at least to let us have the answers to the questions that were being asked. We were all afraid to fall in Russian hands, but for the time we were full of trust that everything was put to rest.

The Crippling Shock

The crippling and shocking news was a time to remember by all. In our village, we had received the message on March 16, 1944, that everybody was to get ready to leave. Packing began, and by morning on March 17 everybody was ready with the horses hitched to their wagons. The gathering spot was just above the village and all were to meet at 7 a.m. The entire village was busy packing their little bit of belongings onto the wagons. Covers were pulled over top of the wagons; there the small children would be sheltered from the cold freezing winds that would blow across stepes. The necessities were gathered through the night. The women were making bread and the chickens were butchered. I remember that night very well, my parents and I we never laid our heads down that night. We worked steadily through the night. My father loaded a small bag of flour on our wagon. We couldn't take too many supplies; there were four of my younger siblings in our wagon. By morning we were ready. My mother had to stay with the smaller children on the wagon. My youngest sister Rosa was only 18 months old. Mother was sitting on the wagon holding the baby wrapped in her *halztuch* (shawl).

Looking Back

The time came to depart. My dad's youngest brother Heinrich and his only sister Rosa were amongst the wagon train. All three families were lined up to leave. Before leaving, my father opened the barn door and the remaining pigs; chickens and cows were free to roam.

We had received orders to leave our home behind. The news was catching up to us. The Russians were pushing with full strength from the east. It had leaked out that the Russians had pushed in the southern part close to Odessa.

Odessa was only one hundred kilometers from our village. It was scary for our own people knowing the Russians were close by. We heard that the German Army had pushed the Russians toward the east. That gives us hope that we were going to go back home again. We never knew how far the Russian frontline was behind us.

I remember before our wagon was set to leave, my father walked one more time to our little home. My father reached up with both his hands, and pressed his weight against the door. He lowered his hands, he turned away from the house and one could see the tears were running down his face. My brother Gottlieb and I stood beside the wagon, crying. We were feeling the pain seeing dad crying. There was no room on the wagon. Gottlieb and I being the oldest siblings had to walk behind the wagon.

At the gathering spot we were divided into groups. Being a close-knit family, my dad's brother and sister wanted to stay with us. A supervisor from the German Army traveled with us. He was there to help us on our journey from village to village.

BK stood for, 17th District boundary. We had received orders to start moving after a signal shot made by a gunshot. The signal was given. The horse drawn wagons started to move on. Rumbling noises were heard as the wheels on the wagon turned, and the horse's hooves pounded on the ground. Along with that you could hear the sound of our crying mothers. It was heart breaking to see whole villages desert their homes. So many tears were never shed as on that day. Nobody wanted to be left behind. The movement of our long wagon train went slowly. It was the beginning of our long journey. On the first day we pushed toward the west. We went as far to our neighboring village of Rohrbach which was our resting spot for the night.

Nearing the village of Rohrbach, we wondered if there would be enough room for some many people. Would there be room for our wagons and horses? As we were entering the village we noticed it was abandoned. Only chickens, dogs and cats, and a few cows are wandering around in the yards. Everything was quiet. They were evacuated before we came. It was arranged that we all could stay in the empty lonely villages. Everything looked so sad. Thoughts went back home, who will be in our homes tonight? Will there be people staying in our homes? If so, they must be going through the same heartbreaking experience. It was well planned. We stayed nights in the empty homes of the villages we went through. Each village deserted like the ones we just left behind. We went through the villages Rohrbach, Worms, Zibeiko, Bergen, Katzenbach, and many more.

Day in and day out, our wagon train kept going. We continued staying in homes that were abandoned. We were getting used to making ourselves at home in the homes of strangers. In our one night home, we began searching for things that was left behind. In the cellars we found sour cucumbers and some barrels of wine. We helped ourselves to everything. We butchered chickens during the night. There was not enough rest; we kept busy gathering supplies on the way. But at this point we were not suffering from hunger. After all, we still had our own bread and meat from our own home that we brought along. We also still had our cow tied to the wagon for our milk.

The nights went by fast. In the morning it was the same routine, pack the children onto the wagons and move on. Depending on the size of the yard, that was how many wagons were designated to that yard. If the house was larger, more people were crowded into it. It gives us a sad feeling to sit in somebody else's home. Everything left behind. These were the home of our fathers and forefathers for generations. They also worked like mules, and now left everything behind. In the corner sat an empty baby cradle. Many times I had to let my emotions go and could not help but cry.

For now, we were still accompanied by the German Army showing us toward the West. We were still on Ukrainian soil. It was like a big dream to us. It sounded like soon we would be out of the danger zone. We were hoping that soon we would be going home. We could not believe that Germany was losing the war. We were leaning on the German Army. It could not be that Germany was losing the war. It must be just a temporary situation that would be cleared up shortly.

Day after day toward the west we traveled. Each day passing, our situation became more and more difficult. Traveling through the rough open country roads was hard on the horses and the wagons. Entering the Moldavian territory, the roads were very poor. Every day the load became heavier to pull for our horses. We started to get stuck in the mud. My brother Gottlieb and I were walking behind our wagon; day after day; from early morning until the evening. When our wagon train came to a stop for the night how it is said in German, "Die lange bringt die last". To admit the longer you drag on the heavier becomes a burden to carry. In spite of all the misery, Gottlieb and I were in dictating a song. We were heard singing alongside our wagon. Gottlieb and I were singing a few verses from the song.

> Out of Russia, we were taken
> All the scattered German people
> No one showed a road of roses
> We were all alike
> Hitched up and heavy laden
> Stood our wagon by our door

Anna Fischer

It's so sad
Our farm and Home stay behind
And as we went over hills and forests
And over fields and times through villages
Bread and water it was without or bitter

Reality set in as we were entering Moldavia. We saw for ourselves that people living there were very poor. The men were taken to the Army or deported for the Russians. Who were left were poor women and children. We had a feeling that our times of plenty of food were at an end. There were no supplies to be found. No feed for our horses. Our food supply was becoming short.

We were driving in mud and often became stuck. In the ditches alongside the muddy roads, you could see dead bodies of prisoners lying frozen under the thin layer of ice. Both sides of the road we were traveling were littered with dead bodies. It was unsightly to see and fear of uncertainty rose. Our traveling conditions became worse. In some areas our wagons sunk into the axles in mud. We were not accustomed to driving for so long in mud. We were not familiar traveling in the Carpatin mountains. We were forced with our route to the high point at the top. Then down the very steep valleys. The men had led one wagon at a time down the steep hills. The back wheels had to be braced with a long tree branch. The men holding back the wagon, easing it down the hill. Wagon after wagon was brought down. Sometimes, it became very dangerous, and the children were taken out of the wagon and made to walk down the steep hills. The little ones too small to walk were carried down the hill. It was very scary and one very slow process. As weeks of traveling passed, our supply of food was running out.

There was nothing to in the poverty stricken countries that we traveled through. The people were showing signs of becoming ill. There was no medication available.

Looking Back

 The week before we had to let our only cow go. She wasn't producing any milk. There was no more feed for her. There was no time for grazing, and we were always on the go. The cow shut down her milk, so we had to let her go in a strange country. She had her freedom, and hopefully found a new home. But for us the time brought only hardship. My baby sister Rosa became very ill and there was not a drop of milk for her. No doctors and no medication. My mother was sitting in front of the wagon holding the little one in her arms protecting herself and baby with a shawl. It was strung over her shoulder kept the chill off the both of them. It was early spring and was cool, especially at night. Sometimes the temperature dipped down to the freezing point.

 My father was leading the horses day after day walking, holding on to their halter. The horses pulling the wagon loaded with the little children and their mothers. My father asked my mother if our little one was still alive. With tear filled eyes, she nodded her head acknowledging that she still was. My little sister laying my mother's arms, her little body looked so lifeless.

 We had a small box in front of the wagon containing a few dishes. Father said to mother, "if the little one perishes we would empty the box, and when the wagon train was stopped during the night, we would put the little one inside the box using it as a casket and bury her". It was impossible to stop during the day with a wagon train. We traveled many miles along the roads. The roads are very congested. We never stopped moving until it was dark. Not only was it the wagon trains on the roads, there were military trucks and marching German soldiers on foot and big troops of prisoners of war. Everything was pushing toward the west. The German army took the Russian prisoners with them. Everybody was looking drained. They all could hardly walk. They were worn out. A young German soldier could barely walk. I noticed a pair of army boots hanging over his shoulder. He asked my father for permission to walk behind our wagon and hung on. This made his journey easier. The young soldier couldn't have been more than 19 or 20 years old, tears streaming down his cheeks. Gottlieb looked at me and we both started to cry. The young soldier must've noticed that I had my feet wrapped in rags having lost one of my shoes in the deep mud. Now, we were all three of us, Gottlieb, the soldier and myself were hanging on to the wagon. By evening, the young soldier had to part and join his troops, but before he left he handed me his army boots that hung over his shoulder. I think it was his way of saying thank you for our kindness.

I was very happy to receive the army boots even though they were way too big for me. My feet became full of big blisters from the booths rubbing against my feet. The blisters were very painful. By evening we stopped in a sheltered area. My mother wrapped my feet in rags. We always had to stop in the forest or in sheltered areas because of air strikes and bombing spree's.

It was dark and we started gathering dried leaves for our poor horses. We were not allowed to make fires for fear of being attacked. Father put the leaves in front of the wagon. He was turned the horses around for them to eat the leaves. Gottlieb and I slept under the wagon. All through the night we had to listen to the noised the horses made. By morning the horses had eaten half moon shaped areas off of the wagon. That's how hungry they were. We had the worries of the wolves coming down from the mountains to attack our horses. We had to protect our only transportation. We couldn't afford to lose our horses. The men had to take turns to stay watch.

Our little baby was still holding on. Mother made some soft Brie for the little one. My mother thought that the little one was improving, but still very weak and half starved. We all were half starved, as there was hardly any food and no feed for the horses. Mother traded her wedding ring for a bag of straw for the horses. My father found the ring. It was not an expensive ring at all, but was the only ring she ever had. Nonetheless, she was so proud of it. Now she had to give it up.

We were traveling day after day not knowing where we were going. We had no idea how long we could endure this kind of life. But we had to continue. Suddenly during the night as many times before, we heard an explosion. In the morning we discovered that the bridge was bombed, and we were rerouted. The next two following day the bridge was restored.

There were some casualties due to the explosion, we heard wagons loaded with people crossing the bridge when that the explosion occurred. When there is war, there are casualties. It was sad to hear of so many innocent lives being lost. We had to struggle for our own lives.

We were close to the Moldavian border when we were ordered to take shelter in the *semelanka* (little mud house).

In the mud house was a woman with a young girl, of about seven years old. The woman's husband was gone, probably taken away. Our men, women and children lay on the floor to rest. We were all packed together side by side on the floor. It was nice and warm in the little house. I let other people find a spot first. My mother along with my younger siblings had settled on the floor. The men again took turns to protect our horses from the wild beasts. Soon everybody had settled and there was no more room for me. There I stood, not even a small spot. The lady that owned the little mud house and her child were sleeping on top of the oven. And there was heat from the oven. The woman saw me standing and must have felt sorry for me, she waved her hands for me to come and take a spot with them. By now, I had a hard time to walk through the packed bodies lying on the floor. I nestled myself on top of the oven with them.

After my father's shift of watching out for the horses, he laid on our wagon. That was his first good night sleep in weeks. The same routine by the signal we had to be ready. We had to take many different routes because the Russians were behind us. We pushed forward toward the west. We hadn't realized how close the Russians were really behind us.

We heard that the Russians had circled some of the other wagon trains. With luck the Germans quickly pushed them back.

For over two months on the run, people were feeling filthy. No facilities to have a bath or wash our clothing. We were all infested with lice, which was brought on by malnutrition, uncleanliness and sickness. We were on the run from March 17 to almost beginning of June until we arrived at the Hungarian and Czechoslovakian border.

Loaded with our wagon train we were directed toward the freight train station in Desh. By arriving at the train station, immediately we were ordered to hand over our wagons and horses to the German Army. We were only able to take what we were able to carry. The rest of our supplies had to stay on the wagon.

On each of the wagons along with the horses, the German soldiers headed toward the eastern front. How far the horses were able to go God only knew. Our horses were to be pitied. It was hard to part with them. But then again, we were relieved that we no longer had to see the horses suffering. Our horses became part of our life. They were suffering with us day and night.

At the train station we were loaded 30 to 40 people in each boxcar. Each boxcar load received several loaves of bread to divide amongst all of us. Being transported by train toward the north, we have no idea where we were going. The train had to stop and change tracks because of the air strikes and bombings. After traveling for hours and finally reached the end of our journey. We now had landed in Poland.

We all emerged from the train, with one short distant walk we were led to a large building. We were all separated, the females from the males. We were ordered to strip naked and stand in line. Our belongings and clothes were placed on the wide movable belt. We one by one were taken through a medical

Looking Back

examination. After the medical exam, we were then taken to the area to be de-loused. Our clothing were disinfected, then tagged and numbered. We were allowed to get dressed again. A short walk led us to the barracks. There again there were no facilities to take a shower or bath. We were not able to wash our clothes. In a couple days we were infested with lice.

The beds in the barracks were full of bed bugs.

It was a miracle for my little sister Rosa to be alive. After going through the medical, she was immediately taken from us and was taken to the hospital in Hohensalza. Her hair had grown on the small of her back because of the malnutrition. In the meantime, we were struggling in the barracks in the city of Krushwitz. A week went by and my younger brother Adolf became very sick. He was nine years old at the time. He was bitten nightly the bed bugs. His blood level became very low. He was so weak he could hardly walk. Upon a visit from the doctor, he was given some medication and some ointment to rub on his body. Hopefully at night he could get rest and recover.

The doctor was explained, "Not everyone gets bitten by the bugs". Bed bugs host only on a certain blood types. Adolf was to the point that red blood platelets were so low that the white platelets almost took over. I felt the bedbugs ran across my face during the night. They were very fast. They never bothered me, was a creepy feeling. They only came out at night. They would hide in the folds of the bunk beds and in the walls of the barracks.

Every day of the cast-iron kettle was filled with water that stood outside the barracks. The water was brought to a boil. The clothing was put into the boiling water to kill the lice. Everybody had lice. They were on our bodies, in our hair. No matter how many times our clothes were boiled, we still had lice.

Every morning a big truck came to the camp. They picked up the younger people. We were taken to open large field of beats to work. We were given hoes and had to clear the fields from weeds. In the evening we were taken back to the barracks. In return the farm owner supplied the camp with beets and potatoes for the camp. Soup was made from the vegetables.

The German personnel were moving people out from the camp into the various places. Some went to cities and others in the country in Poland. Every day there was a steady stream of people coming into the camps in Krushwitz and many other camps. My Aunt Rosa's family received orders to get ready to leave the camp. They were taken to the train station in Krushwitz. They were placed on top of a load it coal. As the train started moving we could hear her calling out to her brother, "Karl, Karl, Karl". We stood at the station crying, waving until the train had disappeared from our sight.

The next to leave was my father's younger brother Heinrich. My father's family was all scattered around Poland. My father wanted to go with them, or maybe close by. He didn't want to be parted from his brother and sister. We were not allowed to go and that was the last time he saw his sister and brother alive.

Days later, our family was notified to be ready. The call came for us to be removed from the barracks. My parents immediately took the train to the Hohensalza Hospital to get our little baby Rose. They wanted her to be with us when we would be taken. My parents fears that if they didn't get her, she would be released and placed in an orphanage. If that happened, we wouldn't be able to locate her ever again.

My mother stretched out her hand to take Rosa from the nurse's arms. The little one tightened her grip around the nurse's neck tight and started crying. Rosa was taken very good care of in the hospital from the nurses. The nurse's loved little Rosa. Rosa had bonded to the caring nurses and didn't want to go with her mother. My sister was a real tiny blonde child. They called her, "Das reine Deitshe kind". She was cute and cuddly and quiet. The nurse holding Rosa started to cry and handed Rosa to her mother.

Looking Back

Now Rosa was with us again. Two days later we had received order to leave the barracks. We were driven to the train station. Our journey was toward the West. It was the middle of July after a long train ride we ended up in another camp in the city of Shwabish Gmund. The camp was full of displaced, homeless people.

Our family was brought to a large building. There were so many people from different countries and different nationalities. We felt lost and alone.

There were many air strikes and bombing sprees. Sirens and planes were heard mostly during the night. We spent most of the time in the barracks than in the open. Sometimes two to three times during the night we had to drag the children out of the bunk beds to run for safety. We were in Shwabish Gmund for approximately one and a half weeks. It seemed like a long time. The food was very poor all we got was a potato, salt and pepper to eat. The potatoes smelt rotten. But if you are hungry you try to eat whatever came your way. We were hoping to get out of this place and find freedom. The war was still going on full force.

We struck luck. A business owner came to the camp looking for employees. Because all the younger, healthier men were drafted into the Army, that left our older men and women to do the hard work. Our entire family was taken into an office there we were questioned. We were asked what kind of work we would be able to perform. Records showed my parents were skilled in farming. I was asked if I would be able to milk cows. We were nervous in answering their questions wrongly. We were looking forward to getting out of the camp. It was dangerous here in the big city. We were afraid of the strike attacks in the sky.

The next day we were called back. Our family was assigned to a business owner of a sawmill operation. The business owner's name was Fritz Kerntner. He had come to pick us up right from the camp. Mr. Kerntner accompanied us to the train station in Shwaish Gmund. He traveled with us, changing trains in Mergendheim. The next stop was Greglingen, and was our final stop.

We were full of curiosity and excitement. My parents were wondering what lies ahead in our future. Now we thought we have peace and quiet. Fritz's wife had prepared us some soup. We appreciated the soup for we were all hungry. After we finished eating, we were led to a small little house with two small rooms and a small kitchen. There were eight of us in the family. Gottlieb just had his 16th birthday. The day was August the First.

I was taken to a small cow farmer, George Balbach in the town of Greglingen. Greglingen looked more like a farm town. I didn't have much to pack as I had only a small bag of clothing. I had so much to learn, cutting alfalfa with the scythe and bring it home from the field. Chop it with the cutter. I never in my life had operated a wagon with a cow harnessed to it. I had to learn how to operate the brake on the wagon so I wouldn't run into the cow. Many times I held back my tears because I wasn't sure I was doing my job properly. Tilling the field with a one-cow harness was hard work for an eighteen year old. It was a big change for me; the cows never came out of the barn. There was no pastor for grazing.

My father and Gottlieb worked very hard at the saw mill. My father found it very hard. He never had the chance to regain his rest. He also found it difficult to understand the different dialects of German. It took some time to understand each other. But with each passing day it got easier.

Even for me at my job, when Mr. Balbach spoke to me I couldn't understand his dialect. At times I felt frustrated. Mr. Balbach said to me, "The devil you want to be German and cannot speak it". I told him to speak to me in the High German and I'd understand. But he just ignored me.

He told to me take the hoe and basket and get potatoes from the field. "Hoe" by him was "*coshed*", for me it was, "*hacke*". "Basket" for him was "*cravle*", and for me was, "*karbchen*".

Looking Back

"Potatoes", for him was "*ebira*", and for me was, "*Kartofel*". I shook my head, I hadn't realized that were so many different dialects of the German language. I was wondering, which was right and wrong? Later o it was said that there were over 300 different dialects of the German language.

We were found work so the refugees didn't end up at the unemployment center. Our wages were low. But it was also hard to find work. We were hoping not to be brought into a bigger city. There were bombing sprees daily. Mr. Balbach was working at the saw mill for good pay. "The Russians", that's what we were called, were working for next to nothing. There were three of us working to support our family. With the war still going, we felt more at peace away from the daily attacks.

By then the bigger cities were in ruins. Things were worsening by the day. We adjusted quickly to our rations. Eating nothing was not new to us. We had the same experience back home in the Ukraine. Food was very expensive; it took the income from the three of us working just to pay for our daily rations. But for the time we were content by doing what needed to be done. People grew more restless by the day. Everybody was walking around full of worry. The last remaining men were drafted into the Army.

In September 1944, Gottlieb received orders to be drafted into the Hitler youth force. My brother had just turned 16 the month before. He was sent to the military training camps in Czechoslovakia, in the vicinity of Budweiss. Now there were only two of us left to work and support the family. As time went by at every month's end, my father asked me, "didn't you get paid"? He was depending on my wage to pay for our rations.

I was a young girl working very hard, with no future. My life was full of worries and concerns. At this time I couldn't visualize a peaceful or a happy future, the only thing in my thoughts was the future of my family. My dear parents who had to go through so much misery, and my siblings, they were all deer in my heart.

Anna Fischer

At that time, there was not a chance for us homeless people. For us the war and hardship was our life. We were expecting to be welcomed in our forefather's homeland, but we discovered the opposite. We were not welcomed. We were called The Russians, hardly acknowledged that we were Germans at all. They could have been proud that we kept our mother tongue, the German language that we had preserved for so many generations. My hope and prayer was that we maintain what we had, and that we can be able to work and provide for our families.

Devastating News

On October 31, 1944, I still recall the disturbing news to me that my mother gave birth to another child. My sister Helen was born. My heart sank; I was angry and was devastated. I thought dear god why? Did we need another soul to care for? Weren't we burdened enough to feed the ones in our family already? Now another mouth to feed! I couldn't find the words to describe my anger and sadness. The most shocking part was that I never knew that my mother was even pregnant. All through our escape and all the run for several months I never knew. I was struggling accept the fact. I felt guilty for feeling the way I did. In my heart my family came first, with many tears and prayers, I found comfort in acceptance of what our family was facing now.

    I felt ashamed at that time having just turned 18 years old, and mother still having a baby. I couldn't face people; I was depressed that I deliberately stayed away from my parents for a while. The little one was part of our family and all turned out okay-- now we were receiving one more portion of our rations because of the little one wasn't able to eat yet, she was being breast fed, so we had more for ourselves.

    Germany had a heavy burden to bear in the middle of the war with thousands of transients, and so many cities in ruins. But our daily work had to go on. It was scary being out in the fields with the low-flying airplanes over us. After working for several months, again my father asked me is if I got paid. It sounded like he was in need of help but I had not received any pay. I never asked for my pay, I was too shy and afraid to ask.

We all shied away from everything and it took time for recovery from our misery. It was very hard to leave everything behind and being so unwelcome by the German people. The only thing left for us to do was work. Upon our arrival in Germany, we were to receive free clothing from the Red Cross.

What I didn't know that Mr. Balbach went and picked up my free garments up at the Red Cross. He in turn charged me a fee for the clothing, which he took off of my pay.

Now winter was approaching and I had to work outside on their small piece of forest, cutting and bundling wood for burning. I became sick and running a fever. I had the flu so I wasn't able get out of my bed. I had not showed up at home to see my family as I usually did. On a Saturday, my father came to investigate and to see why I was not coming home. When my father arrived, he was led to my small corner right under the brick roof. My father could not believe that I was sleeping in such a cold spot--the roof was covered in ice crystals.

My father got angry and said to me, "get dressed, I'm taking you home". He told Mr. Balbach said that if he didn't have a better place for me to sleep then he would take me home. Mr. Balbach told my dad that when he was young, he had to take hot bricks to warm up his bed. Mr. Balbach decided to give me their spare bedroom where it was warm and dry. As soon as I recovered, I was told to go back up to the attic again. A few more months went by without any pay, but I felt powerless. Now, eight months went by and finally Mr. Balbach came up to me one day with a piece of paper in his hand. He came to pay the monthly wages he owed me. He said, "Ya, Anna, you would get 3 D MARK, but I will give you 5 D MARK". I was in shock-- 5 D

Looking Back

MARK for eight months of hard work! I took the money, shoved my few garments into a bag and went out the door.

Crying, I was walking in disbelief toward my parents little house. As I came to my parents, my father asked me what had happened to make me cry? I stretched my hand out toward my father with the 5 MARKS in my hand. My father instantly realized what had happened, but we couldn't do anything. Mr. Balbach and my father's boss at the saw mill were using us poor homeless people. Hardly paying us the wages we were promised and deserved.

My father said to me, "you're not going back to the Balbachs, tomorrow morning you are going to the unemployment office at the City Hall and ask for a different place to work". The next morning at the entrance of the City Hall, a farmer by the name of Fritz Gerlinger approached me saying, "Anna, I had heard you are looking for work." Mr. Gerlinger told me he needed somebody to help his family. "I will pay you 50 D MARK a month, but we have six children to care for. If you would like to work for us, you don't have to go into the unemployment office". I accepted right away, telling him that I would be at his place right in the morning.

I didn't shy away from work, and by now I knew all the farmers in the city by name and the people knew me. I was always friendly and kind. The first day on my new job, my father was let go from his job at the saw mill. They were trying to scare us, and we were scared. Now with dad out of work, that would leave only me to support our family. Father went the next morning to the unemployment center asking for help. After questioning him, they told him that there was no reason for losing his job. Father was ordered to go back to his job. But father said it was never the same after he came back. There was friction because my dad's boss and Mr. Balbach were working together. Now, Mr. Balbach couldn't work full time at the saw mill and had to do his own work on his farm.

Anna Fischer

When I arrived at my new job, Mrs. Gerlinger told me that we had a lot of work. After the cows were milked and the outside chores were done, the house needed to be cleaned. By evening, I sat mending and patching the children's stockings, cleaning and polishing the children's shoes for the next school day. I felt welcomed; I was even allowed to sit at the table with the family at mealtime. It was a big change for me to be included in the family. Working for the Balbachs-- I was fed potatoes from a big iron kettle that was used to cook potatoes for the pigs, and a little spoonful of cottage cheese during the evening. During the day I was given jam bread. Not once in the eight months I spent working for them did I eat with them or had even seen them eating at the table.

My new employers were much friendlier. Mrs. Gerlinger was at home economist. Her name was Hedwick. Right from the beginning she said to me, "Anna, we are going to work this way: one Sunday morning, you will take the children with you to church, and the next Sunday, I will take the children to church. Somebody will be at home preparing the dinner for the family". Mrs. Gerlinger told me this way I would learn how to cook. I thought that was very nice of her and we were all like a big family. This I was included at every meal and I felt at home.

Greglingen was not a big city; most were farmers. After a short time, a course was begun for milking cows. Mrs. Gerlinger said to me, "Anna, take the course, it would be good for you." I had been milking cows since I was eight years old so I didn't care about the course, but Mrs. Gerlinger paid for the course and sent me to it anyway. I learned many helpful things in the course and because the Gerlingers' were well known in town, their barn was chosen to perform the courses. The Gerlingers' were very excited to see the advertisements about it in the papers.

After that, it didn't take long; another course came up. The next course was to learn sewing. Once again Mrs. Gerlinger wanted me to take the course. I remember her telling me, "Now

Anna, this will be good in the future for you; every woman has to know how to sew, and I'm sending you". Mrs. Gerlinger told me that in her younger years she took every course that came up and she never regretted any of them. I didn't refuse and I took the sewing course because I never had the chance to sew with a sewing machine before.

The course was held at the teacher's home. Her name was Mrs. Lange. We were a nice group of girls from many of the neighboring farms, and I really enjoyed the sewing course. I worked hard because I wanted to repay the Gerlingers' for their generosity. Mrs. Gerlinger was very sympathetic towards me. She listened to me while we were sitting and doing work for the children. I told her about our life under Stalin's rule and I could feel she took everything in, even though Germany had its own suffering.

Daily, trainloads of immigrants from all over came streaming into our area looking to be free. There escape was from the Russians in the East. The people came from Besarabian, Hungarian and Romania. They had come from all walks of life. They all needed shelter and food. Germany was under pressure and getting squeezed from every direction; there was nowhere to go. Trains arrived daily bringing more homeless children from the bombed out cities. Families were forced to take these children in, having been abandoned or orphaned. By now the German people had lost all confidence in winning the war. The war situation was no longer broadcast. The German People's lives went on only by speculation.

On May 8, 1945, it was officially announced that Germany had surrendered. The war was now over. I found the German people, including our selves, very relieved and hoping our loved ones would return home. At the same time, the German people were struggling with heavy hearts to accept that Germany had lost the war-- especially the younger generation that was brainwashed by Hitler saying, "We shall never give up."

And now we were facing the reality. There was nothing we could do but wait and see what the future would bring to the shattered country-- its people in despair and searching for their missing children and families. The German Red Cross was working around the clock looking for our missing loved ones. There was hardly a family that didn't have someone they were looking for. Our own family was in the same situation. We didn't know where our own were stranded. My father's brother and sister and their families were left behind in Poland. My brother Gottlieb was also missing as the German soldier. There were many worries and sleepless nights, but we never gave up the hope for that one day we would be reunited with our loved ones. Our hopes and prayers gave us strength to carry on day by day.

We knew we had to have patience after the terrible war; it would take time to recover from the mess Germany was in. We had to face a hard and long struggle. The Red Cross was working constantly with so many German civilians, displaced and homeless people and those in prison camps... to help them find information about where many of the their loved ones were captured. There were thousands of things to be discovered.

The Overwhelming News

After searching for approximately one year after the war came to an end and was lost, our family was all in tears after receiving news from the Red Cross that my brother Gottlieb was still alive. He was a prisoner of war in France. It stated that Gottlieb Roth was captured on April 14th, 1945, in the heart of Germany in Frankfurt am Main River. Gottlieb was taken to France by a train full of prisoners. It stated an address:

Comieles Paris c/o Department 221

Prisoner Number 901-801

What a relief just to know that Gottlieb was alive. We were lucky where we were Western Germany; it was easier to search for someone than it was in the East. My parents were praying to get some kind of message. Prisoners were prohibited to write or send messages home for a whole year until everything was more settled. My parents kept close track--the time was getting near for messages to get through. Knowing Gottlieb was alive was a comfort for all of us. The restriction was lifted and the prisoners were allowed to correspond with their loved ones. The wait was long and nerve breaking. Day after day mother waited for the mail to arrive. It was disheartening when the mail carrier passed by.

Anna Fischer

I remember the first letter we received from my brother from France. We were so happy we were all crying for happiness. All this time, not knowing where he was. We were hoping and praying that he wouldn't fall into Russian hands. We were hearing of the Russians cruelty. My brother wrote that the French at the River Main took him as a prisoner of war. It was not too far from where we lived. The prisoners were loaded onto trucks in the night and taken into a barbed wire camp between Germany and France, on the border. Gottlieb told us that out of the 20,000 prisoners in that camp, he was the youngest, at 16 years old. Gottlieb had suffered in that open camp, with only one blanket. The prisoners dug holes in the ground for shelter. A soldier pull away Gottlieb's blanket during a heavy rain, then he lay in the mud. Gottlieb was taken in a short time to a French farmer. When he arrived at the farm, three German soldiers were already employed there. Gottlieb said that the very first thing that the German soldiers asked him was, "Have you got lice?" Gottlieb stood there in his uniform and said to his comrades, "No, I have no lice, the lice have me"! Immediately, Gottlieb was stripped naked and given potato bags to wrap around his body. A German prisoner took Gottlieb's clothing and uniform and put it all into a big boiler filled with boiling water. Gottlieb's clothing was ruined; his clothes had shrunk in the boiling water. He had to wear the potato bags like all the prisoners had to.

The prisoners were sent out to the fields to work. With just the potato sacks wrapped around their waists, none of the prisoners had shirts to wear. The heat caused severe blisters on their backs. There were many painful, sleepless nights.

The German Red Cross was sending donated clothing for the prisoners in captivity, but the black market was very strong. The clothing intended for the prisoners was picked up by the French farmer and sold. The prisoners got nothing. But soon the prisoners heard that they had been cheated out of their share of clothing. They decided to refuse to work in the fields. The French farmer got the message and in the next few days they received clothing to wear.

Gottlieb spent three years in the French prison. Shortly before Christmas in 1948, Gottlieb was released from captivity and came home. We were all glad to be reunited as a family again. I still can recall the happiness of my parents when Gottlieb arrived. He was also introduced to a new sister, Helen, who he wasn't even aware of. Helen was born one month after he was drafted into the German army in 1944.

My parents had found out that an S.S. man had put his 19-year-old son in hiding to avoid being drafted, but in order to fill the quota for draftees Gottlieb was taken. The S.S. man knew we were newcomers and afraid and he got away with it.

After Gottlieb's release from prison, he started working again with my father at the saw mill for Kerntner. While in Germany, we tried hard to fit in with the German people. We had come back home-- the home of our forefathers' birthplace-- Germany. We were strangers in the Germans' eyes but we tried very hard to accept and what ever came our way. It was said by our forefathers, "With a stick in your hand, you are leaving the homeland for Russia. The time will come that you are forced, with a stick in your hand, to return to Germany." The prophecy was fulfilled.

At times we felt depressed; we asked ourselves what we could do? It was not our fault; we didn't start that terrible war. That war brought so much misery to the human race. Of millions, only a handful survived Stalin's criminal acts and WWII.

One thing was clear in our minds-- never, ever to return to our own birth land in the Ukraine. If we would have to choose between returning, and death, we would choose death. Thinking back to the terrible times we had to suffer-- hunger and starvation, at least here in Germany we were supplied with our ration cards.

The Heartbreaking Search

My father had received word through the Red Cross that his youngest brother Heinrich was wounded and in the hospital. Immediately, my dad wrote to his brother in the hospital. In the meantime, uncle Heinrich had found out where his family was. He had been released and was trying to join them. Heinrich's wife, Hulda, had fled from Poland with one horse and a small wagon loaded with their seven children. It was in the month of January in 1945; it was very cold. Three of the children were sitting on the wagon and with their legs hanging off the edge of the wagon. There wasn't enough room for all of them inside the wagon. Because of the freezing temperatures, the three of the children who had their legs hanging over the side had their feet frozen badly. Two of them, from Heinrich's first marriage, were taken to a hospital. The third one child, the youngest, Hulda wouldn't give away out of fear that the child would never be found again.

Looking Back

Hulda had landed in the northern part of Germany, just across the Polish border. Uncle Heinrich was worried about his missing children.

My father wrote one letter after another but there was no answer from the entire family. My dad was full of despair, but he didn't give up. He kept writing to the same address. In his letter he pleaded to whoever opened the letter, "reads these lines, please, I'm looking for my brother and his family." It still took many more letters, but finally he received a reply from the northeastern part of Germany.

The Farmer wrote to my father:

'Dear Mr. Roth…I am sorry to inform you that the family you are enquiring about is no longer here.' He also wrote that the father of the family was released from the hospital two days later. By night, the Russians were freely crossing the border. They came and took the whole family away and didn't know where they were taken. He also wrote that he had spoken with my father's brother and that he was very worried about his missing children. He was going to try to find them through the Red Cross. He continued, writing to my father, 'Mr. Roth, I am sorry, that is all I can tell you about your brother Heinrich and his family.' From that moment on, my father knew exactly what had happened. He knew that he would never see his brother again.

My father had no other choice, but to start the search for his brother's two children, Amalia and 'Little' Gottlieb. My father thought he would do what ever he had to do for his brother. He was taking a huge load on his shoulders.

Through the Red Cross, we were informed that the two missing children were in the Russian zone, and that Amalia was released from the hospital. She was taken in by a German family because she because had no parents. A short time later, 'Little' Gottlieb was also released from the hospital and was taken into an orphanage located in the eastern Russian zone.

In the beginning, the Russians made it difficult and dangerous to cross the eastern border. It was heartbreaking for us in the West to watch the Russians celebrating victory. The Russian Army sat on the border with their American equipment, showing off their achievement of winning the war. And the allies were watching their parades.

In my opinion, the Western world was too easy. The Russians were given too much freedom-- they were crossing the Western border freely, torturing, raping, molesting, taking what they wanted and pulling innocent people into camps to deport them. The Russians should have been ashamed, showing off their victory with American equipment. Russia owes the West an apology.

In The Book "Krushev Remembers" It Is Written...

'Mikoyan confirmed after his trip to America, that they received military equipment, ships, and many supplies from the Americans. All of which greatly aided us in waging the war. After Stalin's death it seems disgraceful how many years have passed since the war had ended, and we still in Russia drive around with American equipment.'

Krushev wanted to stress how many cars and trucks they had received from the Americans. 'Just imagine how advanced our country would have been from Stalingrad to Berlin and Vienna. Our losses would have been colossal, if we wouldn't have had any more maneuverability.'

In addition he said, 'we had received steel and aluminum, from which we made guns and airplanes. Our own industries were shattered and partly abandoned.'

Looking Back

Krushev also mentioned the large quantity of food products they received, he could not give the figures, they never have been published; they are all locked up in Mikoyan's memories.

Now, after the war, there were many jokes going around in the Russian Army--some about the American 'Spam'-- it tasted sooo good! Without American 'Spam', how would we be able to feed our Army; they had lost the most fertile land in the Ukraine. The Soviet Army had virtually no more mechanized transports. It was with the American and British trucks that they were able to advance swiftly and complete the encirclement of the German forces around Stalingrad. And the rapidly sweep across the steppe to shatter the German armor onto Berlin and Vienna.'

When I think of it, I cannot help to feel angry. As the Russians were pushing with great speed into eastern Germany, full of greed to gain the biggest part of Germany, they knew they had it made. They went at it like vultures, with no conscience, still with their allies' equipment. Entering East Germany, they immediately started to dismantle all the big factories, hauling it into Russia.

They rounded up by force, German engineers and technicians to build factories in Russia with the German technology. The Russian technology wasn't as advanced as the Germans. Without the help of their allies, millions of our loved ones would still be alive.

The allies were too easy on them. At the time the Russians were laughing and making fun of it.

Again, focusing on trying to get my Uncle's two children out of the Russian East zone. Amalia stayed with a young lady by the name of Inge after her release from the hospital. In the fall of 1946, Inge had the opportunity to secretly cross the border into the western zone. She was able to bring our cousin Amalia with her, bringing her to our family. Ms. Inge was also fleeing from the Russians to stay in the West. It worked out very well; Inge stayed with us for a short time until she located her friends and relatives. Now, my father was glad we had made his best start. Now, we had one of uncle Heinrich's children with us.

But there was still 'Little' Gottlieb. It was confusing, there were so many Gottliebs in our relationship; every one of my father's brothers had a son by the name of Gottlieb. The one I am speaking of was uncle Heinrich's son. My father was now concerned about 'Little' Gottlieb. He was worried, how would it be possible to bring a small boy out of the orphanage, and cross the Russian zone into the western part of Germany-- we were living under the American occupation.

Our families were the first immigrants--'Fluchlinge'-- who had come to Greglingen from the Ukraine. In a short time, we met at lady by the name Ida Hoffman. She was settled with her children in a small farmer town of Reinsbrun, only a few kilometers from Greglingen. We became close friends. Ida's husband was also missing in the German army. Ida made several trips toward the East zone to visit a lady friend of hers. My father told Ida that he was looking for a child in an orphanage in the East.

By searching, it just so happened that the location of the orphanage was not far away. Ida told her lady friend that my father was very worried about the little child. She asked her friend if there would be a chance to get the child out of the orphanage and across the border. Her friend replied that the only way was through bribery. German money was of no value and could buy nothing for it. Food and ration cards played at big part in the bribery method. The black market was strong.

We received care packages from the church missions, organizations in the USA, and also from some of our relatives in North Dakota, USA. Our family welcomed these packages with open arms. Our father decided to give up some of our food packages to get 'Little Gottlieb' out of the Russian zone before something happened and was too late. Every time Ida went east, we had saved up two or three packages to send along with Ida in the hope of bringing Gottlieb out of the orphanage and home to us. This was not the end.

After several attempts and nothing happened, my parents became suspicious. We never knew if we just were being used, and our packages ended up on the black market. But, our father was not about to give up, saying that we had to do as much as we can with everything in our power. We also had to provide Ida with some of our food provisions and that took its toll. We almost hit the bottom that left our family with no food. It was sad when mother only could bring boiled potatoes to the table and nothing else. Ida could also see we had almost hit the bottom. My father still said he would not rest until he reached his accomplishment. Ida again was preparing her trip to the eastern zone.

The Search Is Over

Mrs. Ida Hoffman arrived unexpectedly in front of our door with 'Little Gottlieb' standing, 'holding onto her hand. Our whole family was overjoyed and very happy. My father stood in front of 'Little Gottlieb' and started to cry. It was very hard; it broke my heart to see my own parents cry. We all started to cry for joy. My father said it was worth going through so many worries and sleepless nights but thanks to God, it was rewarded. What a relief for my parents that the children of my father's youngest brother, Heinrich, were safe with us.

We were shocked to discover that 'Little Gottlieb' had both of fronts of his feet amputated. He was walking on his heels, trying to balance himself. Immediately, my parents were concerned about his future, but for now we were a family-- a large family of 11 people. We had to do what ever we could to stretch the ration cards along way by working together. Once in a while, my mother received a loaf of bread from the bakery, and the shoe store had given a pair of shoes for the children. By now the German community recognized us more than they ever had before. They realized that our family was working from the first day we arrived in Germany. By now, there were so many Fluchtlinge--immigrants, homeless, and nobody working and

Looking Back

not even inquiring for work. They were all on welfare, sitting and waiting for handouts, and the German government was broken down and broke.

We were all depending on foreign countries to help the hungry people. Germany was in ruins, nothing was working and on top of this, the country was being split into four parts. Russians in the East were robbing, stealing what ever they could unscrew. We were feeling very lucky to be under the Americans. In my father's mind, it was still not the end. He was telling us we still have a long way to go in uncertainty, but, we have to have faith and work together and we would make it. But in the mean time, my father was very concerned about his brother Heinrich. My father wished that he could have been able to let his brother know that his two children were safe with us.

Everything seemed hopeless. My father's sister, Rosa, along with her family, were still missing somewhere in the troubled world. We heard heartbreaking stories about the Russian Occupation Zone and Poland. How brutally they treated the Germans. As well as thousands our Germans from Russia. They all had suffered so much. The treatment was so inhumane.

After many years of searching through the Red Cross, finally we began to receive in Germany, messages from our surviving loved ones in Siberia. But it took time for them to be granted permission to correspond with the Western world. Our poor people were hauled out into a godforsaken world.

It was in the winter of 1945, we were waiting to hear something from our loved ones. It took at least 10 years till we would hear messages coming out of Siberia, Archangel, and the Ural Mountains-- all scattered throughout the coldest northern parts of Russia.

Every spare minute was spent searching through the Red Cross for information.

For us, it was heartbreaking to hear about their suffering. We felt for them but our hands were tied, we were still in Germany struggling. But thank God, our family was saved from the deportations. At this time my father was also searching for his sister Rosa and her family. We were almost sure that they were not able to flee toward the west because her husband Heinrich was a sickly man. They had been taken out of the camps and resettled in Poland by the Germans. They had made the whole trip sitting on top of the train's coal wagon.

Hulda wrote to us years later.

> We were being chased out to work like a bunch of animals. All you heard in the early morning was the sound of the speakers throughout the barracks, "Daway, Dawway". (Go to work). We were forced laborers along side the P.O.W.'s.

My dad was glad to hear from our loved ones; at least some are still alive. However, they were in great need. They informed us of their terrible situation, but there was nothing we could do to give them the help they were crying for. My father would have taken that piece of bread out of his mouth and given it to them if he only could have. Our family was struggling at the time in Germany with 11 people. The only thing that saved our lives was the few care packages received from the USA. My father said that if we could have spared some of our tokens that we received, he would have sent them to help our relatives. But, it was not safe at the time, and the shipping cost was very high. We could not afford to spare the goods and pay for the shipping because we had no money either. And on the other hand, the poor people would never have received the packages anyway.

It was rumored that people were warned not to send anything. After the war had ended, Russia had isolated itself from the Western world and there was great famine in the Ukraine. The Russians didn't want the rest of the world to know about it. In 1946 and 1947 they suffered one of the biggest droughts they ever had and this contributed to the starvation in Siberia. There was no food supply left and Russia was covering this up.

With 11 people in the family, we appreciated every little bit we received from overseas; and we were thankful to a very special and kind man by the name of Emanuel Pflugrath. His address was 313E - 5 Ave., Ritzville, Washington, U.S.A. Mr. Pflugrath got our family name and address through his Church in Ritzville.

Church organizations were working with churches throughout Europe and abroad to help the thousands of displaced and homeless people. My family was on one of the receiving lists. Mr. Pflugrath sometimes sent us a package of coffee--that would be a real treat for us. We never had coffee before, but we never opened it, but sold it on the black market to a German dentist for 360 D MARK. With that money we bought potatoes and bread.

Fortunately, I was working for a farmer and sometimes I was able to buy a sack of potatoes. The rest was still bought with the ration cards. My father was starting to struggle with the future for all of us, even visualizing how to build a future for his children. It seemed almost impossible in Germany. Right after the war, cities were starting to be rebuilt. Everything in the big cities was in ruins. There was so much damage from the war. Many homeless people, it was a terrible situation.

My father and Gottlieb were still working at the sawmill. My youngest brother Adolf was working at the same sawmill as a furniture apprentice with very little pay. Unfortunately, for me, with heavy lifting I was hurt and was admitted to the hospital in Creglingen. I had to have an operation. The advice from Creglingen's only doctor --Dr. Schoff-- was that I was not able to work or do heavy lifting after my recovery. I was forced to find a different job.

At that time, I befriended several immigrant girls, or refugee girls. Even though we had received our citizenship papers from Germany, we were still classified as refugees. We still felt lost; the only difference being that we were living in a free country.

After the war, the country was left in ruins. Most of the girls I had befriended had left for a bigger city. While I was recovering from my operation, Mrs. Gerlinger came to see me at the hospital two times a week. She was hoping that I would come back to work for them, saying to me that she would give me lighter work to do. It was hard for me to refuse the offer. She was so good to me. The doctors told me that I wasn't able to do any lifting anymore.

All the courses Mrs. Gerlinger made me take were very valuable to me in later years when I had established my own business. I was so grateful to her and that is why it was so hard to tell her that I wouldn't be coming back to work for them. Mrs. Gerlinger understood and wished me the best in finding a good job in Stuttgart. I thanked her for doing the best for me and treating me like one of the family.

After my recovery at home, I was eager to work and to see my two friends--Teresa, a Hungarian German, and Hermina Zeiser, a Bessarabian German girl.

It was on a Saturday morning that I boarded the bus. With a small suitcase in tow, I was headed for Stuttgart. Arriving at the bus depot, Teresa was already waiting for my arrival. I knew I had to stay over the weekend, but I had no money. Teresa told me that I could stay with her, as long as her boss didn't find out--he wasn't kind toward immigrants. We were still called "Russians". "What did you come here for, to eat our bread? We haven't got enough for ourselves". What could we say or think? We had to be quiet.

On the Sunday morning, after Teresa finished work, she came up into the small room where I was staying. She brought me a sandwich. Teresa was free till Monday morning, and I was anxious to find work. We went to meet more of our "fluchtling" girls. We liked to be in the big city of Stuttgart. We never complained of the hard work and very little to eat. Later in the evening we made our way on foot, and walked for miles on our way to Teresa's work place. Teresa pointed to the "Arbeits-Amt (unemployment center), I was happy to be able to stay at Teresa's little room. In the morning Teresa and I went down to work, but I had to hide. Teresa was telling me the German people didn't like us. There was hardly enough food to feed the German people. Now thousands of immigrants and all homeless were in Germany. We young German people worked hard for very little money.

I walked the street to the unemployment office, searching for a job, to afford food. I was happy to find a job at 22 Schickard St. for Doctor Albert Bogner. The job was available in approximately 3 weeks. His help was quitting at that time. Now for me, where do I go from now on? I had no money and no food. I had no other choice but to go back and inquire for any job to start immediately. I was lucky to find a job for the Seitz family. Mr. Seitz was the headman for the Dimler Benz Automotive Industry in Stuttgart. Now I was hoping to make enough money for something to eat.

I also had given Doctor Bogner the address of my parents and the address where I was working till the time came for me to work for the Doctor. I had kept it a secret from the Seitz's that my work with them was only temporary.

It was in the winter of 1948, and I arrived at my new job at the Seitz's. Mrs. Seitz was organizing the work she wanted me to do. They were living in an apartment suite that I had to clean.

Mrs. Seitz slept in late in the morning. She got up and took her three-year-old daughter out for breakfast. Spending most of her time in the Bath Halle (swimming pool). Lunch and supper was with the family. I never saw them all day. In the evening they returned, sitting enjoying their drinks and reading the newspaper. I was sitting in their small kitchen waiting till they decided to go to bed. Their living room was also their eating area, which also was my hidden sleeping area.

Anna Fischer

My orders were to get up early, hide my bedding, and clean everything away. Boil 1 egg, 1 slice of bread and a small portion of butter for Mr. Seitz. Mrs. Seitz was covering up that I was sleeping in their living and eating area. Mr. Seitz was made to believe that I had come to their residence early in the morning for my day of work.

I had the same routine of dusting, cleaning the scatter rugs on the middle of the floor. I had to go on my knees and straight comb the fringes on the rug. They were to be perfectly straight.

The little cooler in the kitchen was empty, with just one slice of bread. I wasn't even sure that it was meant for me. I was to the point where I was driven by hunger. I eat what was in the cooler. I noticed every day the same slice of bread for the day.

In the meantime Dr. Bogner sent me a letter addressed to my parents address. He thought that I was waiting to hear from him. The girl that was working for him was quitting a little earlier than expected. My father read the letter then sent it to me at the Seitz's address. As soon as it arrived, full of excitement, I read the letter. Doctor Bogner informed me that his girl was leaving earlier. I received the letter on a Friday, and I went to visit my friends for the weekend.

I had the letter hidden in my knitted gloves. While I as gone for the weekend, Mrs. Seitz went through my belongings, and found the letter.

I had stayed at my girlfriends place, and hid there until the next morning. Monday morning I went to work as usual. As soon as Mrs. Seitz got out of her bedroom, she told me that I was fired. I was to leave immediately from my job. I left without Mrs. Seitz paying me a penny. I had worked for the Seitz's for two weeks with no pay and almost starved with hunger in those few weeks.

For me it was ok. I was anxious to go on to my next job with Dr. Albert Bogner. I was hoping desperately to have a job with better working conditions and also getting something to eat. I had no money and I was so terribly hungry.

I took my little belongings, now I was out on the street. I had nowhere to go with no money. I decided to go and see Dr. Bogner, hoping there would be a way that I could stay. I could not afford to go home where my parents were living in Greglingen. I explained to Dr. Bogner what had happened and that I was in a terrible situation. I asked Dr. Bogner if there was any way that I could stay till the time came to start to work for him. I was telling him that I had no money and no place to go.

Dr. Bogner said that I could stay with their maid and she would show me what has to be done every day. That was the greatest help for me. The doctor's assistant was happy to be leaving her job earlier, that I was replacing her. The office that I will be working at took up one complete floor of the apartment.

My room was on the top floor. Early in the morning I took the stairs down to the second floor. I started the fireplace in the waiting room. Dr. Bogner was a throat, nose and ear specialist. I was preparing the sterilized instruments out on the table for Dr. Bogner. By nine in the morning the office was ready for his patients.

Dr. Bogner and his wife, Dr. Bogner Frank were separated, but both had their practice on the same floor. I was very busy answering doorbells and in between sterilizing the instruments. My nicest day was washday. There were no automatic washers or dryers. There was so much laundry to do. The white doctor coats had to be boiled, they had to come out snow white. The soiled pieces had to be rubbed on the washboard.

All the wash was to be hung on the line to dry. I loved my washday. I even had a sandwich brought out to me. It also gave me peace and quiet from all the hustle and bustle in the office. What I liked the most of all, Dr. Bogner's mother was doing all the ironing. She was close to her 80's. Dr. Bogner's parents and his brother Arnold lived on the same floor.

Dr. Bogner had brought his parents out of Poland years earlier. They originally came from Bessarabia. According to Hitler and Stalin's agreement in 1939 to get out all the Bessarabian people out of Bessarabia and settle them in Poland. The Bessarabian Germans were settled in Poland. At the beginning the Bessarabian people were demanding the same homesteads, as they had to leave behind. Hitler was chasing the Polish people from their homes and farms, to settle the Bessarabian people in their homes, in some occasions the Polish people had to work for the Bessarabian people that had belonged to the Polish people before. That had created a lot of hatred against the German people. You could not blame the Polish people, the only thing by regaining the power with the Russian occupation. Many of our innocent people had to suffer under the unjust circumstance.

No wonder the Bogner's parents had to be taken out early enough to save their lives. The home that the Bogner's lived in originally belonged to a Polish family. The Polish lady was working for the Bogner's in her own home that was taken away form them. Mrs. Bogner was telling me that if her maid didn't do as she was told, she would take a whip after her. Mrs. Bogner was laughing as she was telling me this. I was speechless, I thought how cruel. Did that mean that this was something she was going to do to me? Was capable of going after me with the same whip? She was a very rough woman. I was thinking how rude she was to her very own husband. He was a very sick man; he had half of his stomach removed. On his doctor's order, he was to drink milk. He had to practically steal the milk from his wife. I only worked one year for the Bogner's in Stuttgart.

Back in Creglingen, my father was working endlessly with immigration papers to get us out of Germany as soon as possible. My father had heard that the allies had signed an agreement with Russia that all Germans that were born in Russia could go home on their own free will. That was why the Russians gathered all the German people by force. It had worked very well for the Russians. Some of our German people committed suicide.

The Russians freely were crossing the ally territory in the middle of the night, and just forced people to go with them into the camps in the Russian Territory. At one point they had come as far as the Schwabish Gmund Camp. This was the center of the Allied occupation; the ally soldiers occupied them. The Russians wanted to remove the Germans. The people started to panic, women started to cry and protest and scream. We are not leaving from here, the only way you'll carry out dead bodies of here. The women were screaming to the Russians, "leave us alone you murders, you took so many people including my husband". The people were hysterical, and thinking of the terrible time they had experienced under the ruling of the Communist Regime. The women were screaming, "You took my husband away in 1937, and he never came back".

The Russians replied, "Well your husband must have done something wrong, we don't condemn people we will take you all home". "You won't take us home, you'll take us to Siberia", the lady screamed. "Ladies bring me the pot with boiling water. I'll scald the Russian pig". An American soldier rushed the Russian solders in to a car and drove away and never came back. The Russians had to quit taking the people by force. The German people did not trust the Russians.

My father was afraid, never knowing what would happen. There was no regulations, no government. He was steady filling out immigration papers, which kept my father busy. It didn't take long, we received forms to immigrate to Brazil, but my father was hesitating to go to Brazil.

My father requested forms to immigrate to Canada. The immigration department was telling my father to immigrate to Canada. The process was easier if you have sponsors who will commit themselves to take responsibility for you. They would have to support you and help find accommodations until you can become self-sufficient.

My father had a brother living in Canada since 1928, and several nephews from a deceased brother. He also had many cousins living in North Dakota, USA. My father's immigration papers were leaning toward Canada. We had no funds, and for us to save that much money to immigrate was impossible. In the meantime, my Uncle Wilhelm in Canada was working to get things in motion. With the help from relatives in Canada, Uncle Wilhelm was able to bring enough money together for 2 people to immigrate to Canada. They also were going to be sponsors for our family in Germany. It was a tough decision to make as to who was going to Canada out of the 11 in our family. My father was very happy that we had a start. It decided at the first opportunity to leave, his nephew and niece were to be the first ones. We could not leave them behind, so father said that when the time came, Amalia and her brother Gottlieb would be the first of the family to leave for Canada.

Finally in 1948, we received a message that the fair to Canada was paid. Amalia and her brother Gottlieb had to go to the immigration center at the Bremen Departure Center. Amalia and Gottlieb had to go through the medical examination center before they would be permitted to immigrate. Amalia passed all the medical qualifications, but Gottlieb was not so lucky. The fact that both of his forefeet were amputated, he did not pass the exam. He was walking on his heels. His waking was very unstable. There were going to need more assurances need from his sponsors. My Uncle Wilhelm in Canada also had a large family and he was reaching close to his retirement age. Now it was uncertain if he was able to undertake the responsibility required to support Gottlieb under his circumstances. It was not known if Gottlieb would be able to have a job and support himself. It was a very hard decision to make. Amalia and Gottlieb arrived back in Greglingen, until further notification for Amalia to immigrate.

Looking Back

When her call came to immigrate, she needed to be at the Bremen landing. She was loaded on the ship in 1949 with many more immigrants. Amalia spent Christmas on the ocean and had arrived in Canada in the New Year of 1950.

My father was glad that a new beginning was made. Now our family was patiently waiting, for what lied ahead of us. Again our family received messages that it was easier to immigrate to Brazil. But my father said we would wait for the chance to immigrate to Canada, but would consider Brazil if there were no other way.

M father started corresponding with relatives in North Dakota, USA, and made them aware of his intentions to immigrate to Canada. Some of the relatives started to pull together to raise money for one person to immigrate. My father came straight out and said that I was to be the next one to leave for Canada. I was the eldest of my siblings. Again we were notified that the money was raised for one more person to immigrate to Canada.

It didn't take long; we received a letter from the Medical Center at Bremen for Little Gottlieb and I to attend. My father again sent Little Gottlieb with me. We both left Greglingen to go to Bremen; on arrival we immediately went through our medical exam. I passed the medical requirements, but for Gottlieb, once again for the second time, did not pass. I would be notified for the departure date.

Gottlieb and I arrived back at Creglingen to our family. My father was heart broken to learn again that Gottlieb was not accepted. I had to wait until further notification, I was not eager to leave my family behind. I was scared going all by myself to Canada over the big ocean. I was afraid to go into the unknown. Into a strange land, and on top of it all, not being able to speak the language. My father noticed that I was very scared, many times seen me cry. It was very hard on my mother and the whole family.

Anna Fischer

My parents told me that this is what we have to do to get out of Germany. My father said it is very unsettled here, and I had to go. Going to Canada meant meeting my dad's only living brother.

I was notified to report at Bremen Hafen Ubersee Heim (at the departure Center at Bremen). For me it was very painful to leave, and leave my family behind. Our family was a very closely knit. It might have been because we had to go through so much misery together in our life. By parting, many tears were shed. My family standing as my train started to roll on. By arriving at the port, there was only a short stay. Our ship was already waiting on shore. It was the end of May and we boarded on the ship. The floor was wide open with rows on rows of 2 tier bunk beds. It was not a fancy ship. Our ship was a Swedish ship called the "Anna Salon".

I was directed to by quarters, Bed #34. The first day on the ship, I became sea sick. And on the second day on the ocean I didn't feel much better and I stayed in my bed.

The sea sickness resulted in many tears, at times it became vary scary, the ship started to sway with the heavy waves splashing against the ship. It sounded like hammering on the ship.

I lay in my bed I remembering saying goodbye to the Gerlingers'. Mr. Gerlinger gave me a bottle of schnapps to settle my stomach when I got seasick. Just to take a sip would help. I lifted my suitcase on my bed. I left my room briefly to go to the washroom. On my way back to my room, I could hardly walk. I was using every bed on the way for support until I reached my bed. I was getting worse, wondering how many days this would go on. I was hoping I wouldn't die on the ocean. I had heard people saying that when one died at sea, your body would be thrown out to sea. I got to my bed. My bottle of schnapps was gone. Someone had stolen my bottle of schnapps. I had a good idea who it was, the neighbor lady was very sick, her son beside her saw me open my suitcase and probably saw it, and took it.

Looking Back

I was thinking to go on deck and get some fresh air. Perhaps I would feel better. The sea air was stale and heavy.

As I made my way back down the stairs, half way down I slipped and fell down the stairway. I was sick, missed my family and couldn't stop the tears rolling down my face. Two sailors came by and helped me to my feet. They started talking have a conversation in German with me. Asking where I was going in Canada. I was told them Richmound. I only knew my arrival address was Richmound, Saskatchewan. They told me how I would like it there, and it was a very nice city. I went back to my bed to lye down for a while. Everything smelt like the ocean, I had no appetite to eat. The crewmembers on the ship were friendly. The dinner tables were nicely covered with tablecloths, and decorated with fresh flowers. The only place that I wanted to stay was in my bed.

While in my bed, I heard crying. I got up and followed the sound of the crying. I found a girl crying, she must have been twelve or thirteen years old. I asked if she is feeling sick, I moved over to her bed, and she told me that her sister and husband had forced her to go over seas. She said her mother was deported to Siberia. I held her hands and told her that when she is in Canada, and if her mother is able to get out of Russia, she would be able to bring her to Canada too. She started to smile, and said that by then she may possibly be a mother herself. I told her that I also had to go alone, and I left my parents and siblings behind. The girl was sick like most of us. We suffered for seven days and seven nights on the ocean. The smell of food made me sick. We were hoping our journey would soon be ending.

Next morning I got up and got dressed. I decided to go on deck when I heard noises. I heard cheering, clapping and shouts of "Hurrah". We finally were sailing toward land... Canada. Someone's voice on the loudspeaker could be heard. Our instructions were to pack all our belongings. We were about to port. All were excited to arrive and the seasickness would be over.

Anna Fischer

We ported in Halifax, Nova Scotia. From there we were led to a big building, "Pier 21". The date was June 4th, 1951. In the big building, we received all our documents. The immigration representatives had greeted us, and were friendly and helpful. After receiving my immigration identification card and train tickets, I was escorted to the train station. I was also given $10.00 so I could buy food on the train. All of my identification cards were pinned onto my jacket. I couldn't speak a word of English. The money I received was of no use to me I thought. I wasn't able to, or wasn't sure how to ask for food. It was difficult for me to communicate.

I was scared and nervous of my new surroundings. By nightfall, I was ordered to come out of the sleepers (sleeping quarters) by a dark skinned man. I was so scared of him. That was the first time I saw a man with black skin. He was the conductor of the train. I was taken into the caboose. There a gentleman was sitting doing some paperwork. The conductor came and brought me a blanket and pillow, and motioned me to lye down on the bench. I feared something terrible would happen to me and I shook my head and said, "No, No, No". The conductor turned and walked away. After some time, the gentleman who was working on his papers started to talk to me. His words were foreign to me and I didn't understand his language. He then started to speak Ukrainian. With my broken Ukrainian, I was able to communicate with him.

Looking back now, I realize the conductor wasn't out to hurt me. He was trying to help me. I was placed in the caboose so none of the passengers would be disturbed during my change of trains in the middle of the night. The conductor was just trying to make me as comfortable as possible. Not being able to communicate, I always thought of the worst possible thing that could happen. Coming out of Stalin's Regime, we were always scared, and this fear still stays with me today.

Looking Back

On arrival of my destination, I had to switch trains. I was told to come out of the caboose. I was sitting on a bench at the Pennant, Saskatchewan train station. The owner of the station restaurant came and motioned with his hands that I was to come in to wash dishes. I was not afraid, as there were several people around. I went in and washed a big tub of dirty dished, and after I was finished, I was brought a huge plate of breakfast. Eggs and sausages! I was so hungry, and it tasted so good. I still had the $10.00 in my pocket that the immigration office gave me.

An elderly man approached me and started speaking German to me. I was so happy to hear the German language in this strange country. He told me that his parents emigrated from Germany in the early 1900's. I enjoyed his company. He purchased a cup of coffee for each of us, and the time passed quickly. The elderly gentleman stayed with me until my train had arrived. I boarded the train to go off to my next destination, I felt uneasy. The people aboard turned to observe what it said on my tags. I felt like I was on display for all to look at.

As I was seating myself on my seat, I noticed three young men with huge cowboy hats on their heads. They were seated in front of me and they turned around to read my tags. Speaking to me in German, they asked what part of Germany I came from. I was answering their inquisitive questions, and I was happy to hear that the German language was spoken in Canada.

In a short time, the conductor approached us and told the young men to turn around and not to speak to me. The one young man turned around and told me they were to leave me alone. One moment later, the conductor brought me a pamphlet to read. I was angry with him for not letting the young men speak to me. I looked at the pamphlet, but it made no sense to me.

I now realize that this was done for my protection, until I reached my destination. I was protected from the beginning right up to the end of my journey. The immigration department had done its job well.

The train chugged on through the barren province of Saskatchewan. This was the province where my Uncle Wilhelm lived. And this is where I was headed. I was looking through the train window. Everything was too different from what I was used to. The farms were scattered like pebbles thrown into the air and when they would land is where a farm was settled. Houses were painted different colors like Easter Eggs. I wondered how these people could make a living in the middle of nowhere. My mind was racing with different thoughts about this new land I was in.

The train was nearing a station, and I heard, "Leader". I remembered the sailor's remarks about how nice the City of Richmound was. The train slowed to almost a stop. I looked at the sign at the station, which read, "Leader". I looked at my tags, and the letters looked the same as on the sign. I was now told to get out of the train. I looked around at my surroundings; there were only three people around. I was expecting a city. The older gentleman out of the three came toward me and asked, "Are you Anna"? My emotions got the best of me and I began to cry. They introduced themselves. It was my Uncle Wilhelm, my Aunt Christina and my cousin Emanuel.

We got into my Uncle's vehicle, and we were off to meet my other cousins from my deceased uncle. We drove into the hamlet of Burstall, Saskatchewan and stopped at a small mud house. The house was filled with relatives of mine, but to me they were strangers. Meeting many family members was quite overwhelming. A nice lunch was served and all had a good time visiting.

That evening we traveled to the farm in the Richmound area. It was too dark to see. We were all tired from all the excitement. I was tired from my journey. I slept in a bedroom where the boys would have slept. The boys were sleeping on the couch.

Morning all was quiet. The morning sun was shining in the small windows of the little wood built house. I felt it was warming up outside and I got dressed and went outside. I walked from one building to the next. The wheat fields were green and lush; which stood 4-6 inches high.

I returned to the house, and I heard my aunt calling out to her sons to get up. They were to go out and start milking the cow. I took it upon myself to grab the milk pail, made my way to the barn to milk the cow. I started to milk the cow and my Uncle came and told me that that was the job for the boys. When I was done with the milking, I brought the milk to the house. My Aunt said, "You didn't come from so far to work". I told her that I did come to work and I have to work to make money to bring the rest of my family to Canada.

My Aunt prepared a nice breakfast of bacon, eggs, and toast. After the breakfast dishes were washed and put away, I was looking around for something to keep me busy. In the porch I noticed several pails. I asked Uncle Wilhelm what it was for. He told me that it was paint to paint the house. The boys were to do that job. I needed to keep busy so I wouldn't become homesick for my family. I took one of the pails of paint, shook it up, and began painting the outside of the house. The house was small and not very high; and in a week I had the whole house painted with the brush. During the time I was painting the house, my mind would wonder off. I was thinking of how wonderful it would have been for my Uncle Gottlieb and Aunt Katherina to see all us cousins from four brothers together. I'm sure that they could see from heaven. Uncle Gottlieb was in his 40's when he died in 1932, from a ruptured appendix. My Aunt Katherina passed away in 1939. They immigrated to USA from the Ukraine, and then settled in Canada in 1911. There was no more land to be had in the USA, and heard that there was plenty of settlement in Canada.

The one-week stay on the farm went by fast, but I felt it was time for me to go on with my life. I wanted to find work and make money to bring my family to Canada.

Back in Germany my father was worried as to what could happen with the agreement made between Stalin and the Allies. He was afraid that the Russian born Germans would be returned into Stalin's threshold.

I had two cousins living and working in the small city of Medicine Hat, Alberta. I asked Uncle Wilhelm if he could take me there to where my two cousins lived in Medicine Hat. Uncle Wilhelm replied, "First we will drive to Richmound to the store, I want to see if we can find something for you. Anna, you were working so hard here this last week". I didn't need anything. I remembered what the sailors had said to me about Richmound. I was excited to see the big city. I asked my Uncle as to how far away this Richmound place was. I was told that it was just a few miles away. As we neared Richmound, I couldn't believe my eyes. Richmound was not a city at all! It was a small hamlet of just a few houses, a school, general store, and grain elevator and a small catholic church. I learned after the years that the sailors were speaking of the City of Richmond, British Columbia on the west coast of Canada.

We entered the small general store. Violet Freitag was the lady working in the store. My Uncle wanted me to pick something that I liked. I knew my Uncle Wilhelm was not a rich man. They were poor like everybody else; they had a roof over their heads and food that they raised, but no extra money to spare. I could see that he would have been disappointed if I were not to find something. He wanted to show his appreciation for all that I had done on his farm. I chose a plastic half apron with attached plastic ruffles bordering the bottom edge. It cost twenty-five cents. My uncle replied, "What a shame, for all the work you have done, for only a twenty-five cent apron". I told him that I didn't come to take his money. Tomorrow my cousin Emanuel was going to take me to Medicine Hat where I could find a paying job.

Looking Back

    I was now in Medicine Hat, and one week had passed since my arrival in Canada. My cousin Amalia was working at the Savoy Café, and my other cousin Kay was working at the Dominion Glass Factory in Redcliff, Alberta. Not far away from Medicine Hat. I found work at the Club Café on 2nd Street downtown Medicine Hat. My job was doing dishes; that was about the only job I could do at the time where I didn't have to speak. I worked split shifts, working only at the peak hours of the day or night. This really broke up my whole day. One evening the cook told me it was closing time. I finished up with the dishes, and the cook was cleaning up his own work area. I started to exit from the kitchen, when the cook told me to sit on the bar stool closest to the door. A taxi was called for me to take me home. Women in those days were not allowed to walk home alone in the middle of the night. The cook went home, and I was still waiting for a taxi that Chris, the boss had supposedly arranged for me. Next thing I knew, Chris started to pull down the blinds on the Café windows. He then went behind the bar and proceeded to pour whiskey into two glasses. He held up the glass for me to drink. I was now real scared. He was trying to pour it down my mouth. I refused, but he kept on trying. Terrified now, I slapped him across his face. . I started screaming, "T A X I", and in a very few seconds a taxi was in front of the door. I ran out of the café and got into the taxicab. I couldn't tell him where I needed to go, so I was pointing out the way to the taxi driver to where I lived. I was crying as I entered my basement suite. Kay came home from her job around midnight. She seen I was crying and asked me what was wrong. I told her what had happened that evening at the café. Kay and I were going to the café next morning. We entered the café and Kay told Chris the owner to pay me right now. He went into the back room and arrived with a cheque, and we left the café.

    After a short time later, we had heard that the same thing had happened to another immigrant girl. We could have gotten Chris in real trouble, but I was so glad to have had my two weeks pay. Back in the 50's women didn't have as many rights as men did. Men seemed to get away with inappropriate actions, and society accepted it. I wasn't out spoken and I shied away from the discrimination about being a displaced person.

My cousin Amalia got me a job with her at he Savoy Café. I was doing shift work and usually worked during the busiest hours. The wages were low, but I managed to save every penny, not even allowing myself to spend five cents. I was saving this money to send for my family.

Back in Germany, my father was working anxiously on immigration papers for Canada. Our relatives in Canada were prepared to help in any way possible. In 4 months time, I had saved $170.00. It was difficult to save any substantial amount with the little pay. I ate at the restaurant for free in my few minutes time off. I was happy to receive the free food. I was able to save the money that I would have to spend to eat. Besides my family still in Germany, so was my Uncle Heinrich's son Gottlieb, who had still not passed the medical.

Our family was fortunate to receive help from the "Lutheran Mission" in Winnipeg, Manitoba, Canada. To our understanding the Lutheran Mission was working together with the World Relief in Europe. Because I was in Canada, it was easier to get help.

Finally the immigration granted my family permission to come to Canada. I was so happy to hear this news. Soon our battle would be over, our goal was soon to be reached, and our wished fulfilled.

I started to look around for a house for my whole family to live in. I found a small basement suite on 12th St. SE in Medicine Hat. It was a small two-bedroom home for a large family to squeeze into.

My parents and siblings arrived in Canada in the fall of October 12, 1951. We were saddened again as my cousin Gottlieb

Looking Back

was once again refused immigration. Our family was welcomed with open arms from all of our relatives. A welcome party was organized for the newcomers. My parents were helped with the necessities, flour, beets, potatoes and other vegetables. It was a great help; winter was just around the corner.

Now finding work for the other members of my family would be difficult. There was the language barrier to overcome, but we found the people in Medicine Hat were friendly, helpful and most importantly, understanding. What was very helpful was that there were many German people living in Medicine Hat.

My family was introduced to the Evangelical Church. The congregation was informed that my father, and my two brothers, Gottlieb and Adolf were looking for employment. We attended church regularly; we got to know many people in the congregation. For the younger members of my family, it didn't take very long to find our way around Medicine Hat. It was a small city in the 1950's. It was harder for my parents to get around, especially for my mother. She was alone at home while all were out looking work, and the younger siblings were at school. I felt sorry for my mother. She kept busy during the day with cleaning, cooking, washing laundry. She was very homesick for back home. Many times we found her crying or tears in her eyes even though her whole family was around. She once said that if the big ocean had not been between the countries, many people would go back home. It was hard for her as she couldn't read or write even in German. She was an adopted child and was never sent to school. She was kept at home to do all the work and chores.

She felt left out on many things because she didn't understand many things around her new surroundings. One Sunday morning sitting in the pew during church service, I noticed my mother holding they hymn book upside down. It was sad to see, I felt like I could cry for her. One another occasion, my mother was not feeling well; she decided to stay home from church. While at home alone and preparing lunch for when we got home, she had the radio turned on. Every Sunday morning, German church services from Winnipeg, Manitoba, "the Lutheran Hour", was broadcasted over the radio. She was so happy to hear her favorite songs sung in German. She though how nice it would be for my dad to her the service as well. She turned the radio off, she thought that if she turned it off, the broadcast would start up again at the same place when she would turn it back on, then we could all listen to the lovely gospel songs. She thought it worked like a record player. As soon as my dad stepped through the door into our tiny home, mother was full of excitement. "Karl, Karl... listen to the radio", she turned the radio on and there was no more German gospel singing. My mother was so disappointed that my father wasn't able to listen to the German songs. She told of how she was trying to save the songs on the radio.

My father had some explaining to do to my mother. Naturally we all had a silent chuckle, but it was sad to see how uneducated she really was. My mother was upset that the radio had let her down. My mother never forgot the humorous incident, nor did we.

The minister from the Evangelical Church on Allowance Ave. S at the time was Reverend Vorath. After we got to know the congregation, through Reverend Vorath, my father found work at the Brick and Tile factory in Redcliff, Alberta; approximately seven kilometers west of Medicine Hat. My father got to work with other workers from the factory.

My sister Hilda worked for relatives on the farm in Burstall, Saskatchewan. My brother Gottlieb and Adolf found work with farmers in the Burstall - Leader, Saskatchewan area, but over the winter months the wages were low, $25.00 per month. They didn't complain, as they were glad that we had food and shelter over their head for the winter. For the remaining 6 people living at home, the small rented basement suite was large enough.

Looking Back

After one year in Canada, and more co-signing from relatives, my father's nephew, Gottlieb was finally permitted to immigrate to Canada. Now finally my whole family was together.

In the spring of 1952, Medicine Hat was hit with a flood with the South Saskatchewan River overflowing. Our small basement suite was under water. A rescue boat was needed to get people out of harm. We lost the little belongings we owned, our clothing, bedding and furniture... gone. Just the clothes that we wore, was all that we had. We once again found a small basement suite on Dominion Street. We made due with the two bedrooms and small kitchen suite for the six of us.

My father worked very hard. He was loading bricks by hand onto the train cars. At the end of his workday, he was completely exhausted, but he had a family to support. My father never complained, knowing that times were worse in his homeland, Ukraine. He was thankful for our freedom, and as long as we were all healthy, that was the most important of all.

A cousin of mine, Ben Roth was working for "Johnson Construction", through Ben, my brother Adolf found work there. Adolf started as a carpentry apprentice at Johnson Construction. He was somewhat familiar with woodworking as he was an apprentice in Germany making furniture. My brother Gottlieb found work at the Brick and Tile with my father in Redcliff.

As for me, I found my second job at "Rabb's Greenhouse". In the fall of 1952, through my cousin Kay Roth, I found that Dominion Glass was hiring. We were always on the look out for better paying jobs. I applied for work at the glass factory. I was nervous at the thought of working there, as I didn't know the language. I received a call for me to work the midnight shift at the factory from 12 o'clock midnight to 8:00 am. The salary was much better than any other job that I had. I was at times nervous about my job; I wasn't always so sure as to what task I was to do. I was afraid that I would be let go because of the language barrier. My job was on the "lare". The glassware was traveling on a conveyor belt, and I was to pick out the defective glassware. It was fast, repetitive work.

Even on Sunday, after church, our minds were busy with work. On Sundays we stored up our energies for the next working days ahead of us. On payday all of our earnings was handed over to our parents. We all worked together as a family to save money for our own home. A bank account was opened and only enough was kept back for living, no extras.

In 1953, after two years in Canada, we were able to buy a small home of our own on 5th street in the Flats area of Medicine Hat. A down payment on the home was made to Mr. Wilhelm Maier. We also made regular payments of $200.00 a month toward the house. My parents were so happy to have our own home. My father proudly walked around the house and told us that with all our help, we all made it possible.

Our little house was not just a house; it was our home. Now in our family there were five of us working. It still took time before our little home was paid off. At the same time the Lutheran Mission was to be paid back for when our family immigrated to Canada. Our cost for the house on 5th street was $8000.00, and in the 1950's it was a large amount of money. We were glad to help our parents to own their own home.

As long as we were still all at home, and working hand in hand, together, we all made it happen. Now we had our freedom. We were satisfied and happy, and we had all the necessities for living, food, clothing and a roof over our heads.

My family was thankful to God for all we had achieved with our hard working hands. Father many times said that we should be thankful to our ancestors who had sacrificed their lives for us, and the next generations to come.

Our family was very close knit. It probably had a lot to do with the fact of the hard times we went through together as a family. It was important to share our feelings, and most importantly, we had each other.

Looking Back

As a few years had gone by, and some of us had reached adulthood, it was time for some of us to be on our own, and leave the nest. This would offer our parents more freedom for each other in their aging lives together. We always were welcomed home for much enjoyed visits.

In the spring of 1955, one of my cousins from Richmound, Saskatchewan, introduced me to a young gentleman that they had known in the same area. His name was Fred Fischer, Canadian born to a German family. Fred's parents and grandparents immigrated many years earlier than when I immigrated. His forefathers were also from the Ukraine, born in the village of Alexanderfeld, approximately 35 km from my own birthplace of Johannestal.

Fred was living with his mother, Mary, on the Philip Fischer farm homestead. His father already had passed away when I first met Fred. At the time I was introduced to Fred, I wasn't excited to meet or even to get involved with someone. At the time I was now 27 years old, missing my teen years during the war, I now was a fully mature woman and had my mind made up that I was going to stay working where I was. I planned on looking after my parents when they no longer could look after themselves. For the first time in my life, I was earning my own income. I was hoping in time, when everyone was out on their own, and our home was paid off, I would live with my parents and look after them.

My cousin Martha Bechtold, nee Roth, came to Medicine Hat for an appointment. They always stopped in at our home. It happened on a Friday when they were in, and I came home from work on my day shift, and I had Saturday and Sunday off. I was having a shift change for the following Monday. Martha asked if I would come out to their farm for the weekend and help her hang some wallpaper. I agreed as long as they would bring me back to Medicine Hat on Sunday night. They agreed and off we went. I helped with the wallpapering, I didn't mind, but I never had any rest either on the farm and by Sunday night we were traveling back to Medicine Hat.

I was told that a young bachelor neighbor came to the Bechtold's farm the following week. They got to know each other when shopping in the hamlet of Horsham, Saskatchewan. Martha told Fred that he should have dropped in at their farm last weekend as they had company from Medicine Hat. A cousin from Russia, and she would make a good farmer's wife. She told Fred that in two weeks, they would be going to Medicine Hat again, and he was welcome to go along to meet this cousin, "Anna Roth", informing Fred that her father and Anna's father were brothers.

Two weeks later, at 4:30 pm, I was just coming home from work, and I noticed that we had visitors. The Bechtold's and this young fellow were sitting in the living area of the house. Suddenly Martha piped up and introduced Fred to me. He had gone along to do some business in Medicine Hat. Martha excitedly told me to get ready; we were all going to the early movie at the Towne Theatre. I had never been to the theatre to watch a movie. I didn't fully understand the language, and secondly, I didn't have the money to go. I still remember the show, "Gone with the Wind". I enjoyed the bag of popcorn that Fred had handed to each of us. After the movie was over the Bechtold's were in a hurry to get back to the farm. . They had left their two small children with her sister and brother-in-law, Louise and Henry Haag. When we reached my house, I got out of the car, and Fred asked when my next day off was. I told him that it would be in two weeks again, and thanked them for the lovely evening. The car disappeared down the street, and I went inside to go to bed.

Two weeks later, on a Saturday, and my weekend off I was planning to sleep in. Later that day I started to clean my bedroom. I just happened to look out of the window, and a truck was parked in front of our home. The truck door opened, and out came a gentleman, and there he stood alongside his truck. I thought that he looked familiar, and thought, yes; it was Fred from the farm. He walked toward our front door. I met him at the door. When the door was open, he asked if I remembered him. I told him that I did and asked him to come inside. My father was sitting at the table reading a letter. I introduced Fred to my father. They immediately hit it off with conversation. My father asked the usual questions, as a father would have. And found it interesting that Fred's parents came from the same general area in the Ukraine. My father was happy to learn that the German language was still used here in Canada, and to keep the mother tongue alive.

I was sitting and listening to their conversation intently, when my mother called from the basement that supper was ready, and all were to come to eat. After supper, I was busy helping with dishes while Fred and my dad picked up the conversation from earlier about our experiences during the war. My dad always pointed out for people to appreciate what they have. The evening passed by quickly, and was time for Fred to head back to Saskatchewan. My father asked how long it took to drive to the farm. Fred said that it took approximately one hour, as it was about 65 km from the farm to Medicine Hat. I went to bed, as the next day was Sunday, and we going to church in the morning.

The following morning my father had mentioned what nice company we had yesterday. My father approved of Fred and said he seemed like a nice man. Fred spoke very good German, and this pleased my father.

On my next day off, Fred came to Medicine Hat. I was surprised to see him so early in the day. Fred wanted to show me a surprise, so we got into the truck and started driving toward the Saskatchewan border. It was obvious to me that we were driving to his farm. When we arrived at the farm, he showed me the surprise. He had natives hired to pick the rocks on the newly broken land. They piled the rocks so they formed a rock wall.

Anna Fischer

This practice was quite common for the Natives, as they were paid by height and width. Fred showed me his land and in the distance we could see the "Home place".

Fred called his mother "Old Lady", and commented that if she hadn't been home, he would have shown me the homestead. I said to Fred, "I think you better stop in, as I'm sure your mother saw us driving around. We better stop to say hello". Fred then drove into the yard and we went into the house. Mrs. Fischer was not surprised that we popped in. Fred was telling his mother that I was German, and I was related to the Bechtolds. Mrs. Fischer was not saying too much, Fred stepped out of the house for a moment. I was left sitting in the kitchen with his mother, Mary Fischer. I felt very uncomfortable. I didn't know what to say. Fred's mother wasn't saying anything either. I was hoping Fred would come in soon. Suddenly we heard somebody driving into the yard. The vehicle stopped in front of the house. Mrs. Fischer hollered out, "Come on in". An older lady came in the house; I was sitting on a stool. I wasn't even introduced to the visitor. The two women were talking non-stop. I heard Fred talking outside to the driver, the driver took off. Fred came in the house saying that we had better go. I was relieved and ready to go. We drove off and Fred was telling me that now the two can talk and gossip all they want, they are two perfect gossipers. I asked who the lady was; that came to visit. Fred declared, "Didn't the Old Lady tell you"? I told him that I wasn't introduced at all. Fred replied, "she's the Old Schafer Lady", the mother my brothers wife, Sally. To me it didn't mean too much. I didn't know the people, but it sounded to me, that they are a bunch of people who didn't get along.

On my day off, I was planning to get a ride to Bechtolds from my cousin. He would drop me off at the Bechtolds, and I was not sure if Fred would come in again. I mailed a letter to let him know that I would be at my Cousin Martha's farm.

Looking Back

Fred had received the message, and showed up at the Bechtolds farm for a visit. My cousin Emanuel was to come the next morning to take me back to Medicine Hat.

That evening Fred went home after his visit. He hung up his cowboy jacket, and forgot to take the note that I had written to him, out of his packet. Old Lady Fischer went through Fred's pocket and found the note. She couldn't read the letter, as she was illiterate. She gave the note to her daughter-in-law to read to her. She wanted to know what was going on and what her son was up to.

After finding out what the paper had written on it, Old Lady Fischer asked Fred how the visit went at the Bechtolds. Fred got mad at her, as he knew then that she had gone through his pockets. He was going to drive up to his sister-in-law to give her a piece of his mind. Now the Old Lady couldn't let it happen that Fred go see his nosey sister-in-law, so that only left the Old Lady confess that she went through his pockets. Fred asked his mother if she now felt better after having read the note, and if she was all that much wiser for it.

Fred came one day to Medicine Hat with his mother. She was going to visit her sister Karoline and her husband Wilhelm Straub. It just so happened that her sister wasn't at home. Fred was coming to visit my family and myself, but Mrs. Fischer insisted she wanted to go home. Fred told her that she had no choice in the matter. He told her to come inside of our home, and she replied, "I'm not going in, I'll stay in the truck".

Fred drove up to our house, and we were all at home. I just so happened to be looking out the window and saw Fred's vehicle and two people were inside. I noticed lots of hand movement as if there were an argument going on. I opened the door of our house and told them to come inside. Fred told his mother that she can now go inside and meet Anna's family, or you can sit in the truck and make a fool out of yourself. Fred had told me of the events going on in the truck later. So finally the truck doors opened and both came out of the truck, walking toward our house door. I saw Fred's mom, and said, "Hello, Mrs. Fischer, it is nice to see you". Fred introduced his mother to my parents. Mrs. Fischer told how she wanted to visit her sister, but nobody was at home. My father, always hospitable, told her that she could visit with them. My father being a very talkative man, curiously asked when they had immigrated to Canada, and informed her that we had come from the Ukraine.

Looking Back

Fred Fischer came to Medicine Hat to visit Anna Roth.

Anna Fischer

Fred Fischer and Anna Roth before they were married.

Anna Roth

Looking Back

ESTATE FARM
AUCTION SALE
to be held at the farm of the late
FRED FISCHER,
HORSHAM, SASKATCHEWAN

2 Miles West of Horsham, Sask. 2 Miles South & 1½ Miles West or 38 Miles N.E. of Medicine Hat, Alberta on Highway No. 41, 6 Miles East and 2 Miles South. Watch for signs.

WED., APRIL 8, 1970, 10:00 A.M.

FREE LUNCH   TERMS CASH

TRACTORS: 1966 Case model 1030 "Comfort King", dual hydraulics, L.P.T.O. P.S. oversized tires, 1322 actual hrs., a big tractor in top condition; Case model 600 case-o-matic with Robin front end loader manure fork and gravel bucket, 3 pt. hitch hydraulics, oversized tires, L.P.T.O.

MACHINERY: 15 ft. Massey Ferguson model 36, wide level with packer hitch; 3 — 5 ft. sections of coil packers; 16 ft. John Deere Surflex 1200 series, with 20" blades, with packer hitch, sealed bearings; 12 ft. John Deere press drill model LLA sealed bearings, solid wheel packers; 24 ft. B1-24 Morris rodweeder; 20 ft. Massey Ferguson model 125 wing type chisel plow; 15 sections of diamond harrows with hydraulic harrow transport on rubber; 12 ft. Cockshutt 240 chisel plow; 12 ft. John Deere cultivator; 4 bottom 14" J.D. plow, 4 new 14" J.D. plow shears; Inland 32 ft. weed sprayer with 150 gal. tank.

TRUCKS: 1961 G.M.C. 3 ton truck completely overhauled, 2 road tanks, real good 900 x 20 tires, 15 ft. grain box, stockracks, McCoy-Renn hoist, V-8 motor, a real good farm truck, 12 x 18' heavy tarp; 1967 Mercury model 100 ½ ton, 352 V-8 motor, 3 speed trans., 16" tires, rear bumper, radio, side mirrors, with 16,000 actual miles, fleetside; ½ ton fleetside Ford, stockracks; 1951 G.M.C. 1 ton truck, good tires.

ANTIQUES: Sask. Lic. Plates dating back to 1931, bed, ice saw, picture frame, butter mold, lantern globes.

COMBINES: 1966 John Deere model 55, self propelled combine with pickup and reels, P.S. varable speed pickup; Cincade straw buncher, almost new.

SWATHER: Massey Ferguson model 30, 16 ft. P.T.O. swather with rubberized canvas.

STORAGE TANKS: 1000 gal. propane tank; 2 — 500 gal. fuel tanks with stands, hoses, nozzles.

MISCELLANEOUS: 4 wheel wide gauge rubber tired trailer with good flat track; MacLeods 17" P.T.O. trailer mounted hammermill with dust collector and pipes; Brandt 36 ft. x 7" grain loader with 12 h.p. Wisconsin electric start engine; 180 amp. electric welder with carbon arc torch; Helmet; Welding rods; 12 ton hydraulic jack; 150 lb. Anvil; Bench grinder; Sioux ½" electric drill; Forester ¼" x ¾" tap and dias set, fine and coarse threads, like new; ¼ h.p. electric motor; 1 h.p. electric motor; Post drill forks and shovels; Craftsman skill saw; 3 hydraulic rams; Comet Hi-Volume air compressor; Beam straightner; Jackall jack; Small tarp; Gas camp stove; Cupboard; 3 cream cans; McClary kitchen range converted to oil; 6 lamp electric brooder; Bath tub; Stone boat; Wagon and header box; Fuel pump; Galvanized stock trough; Feed troughs; Cistern pump; Blacksmith forge; Oil chicken brooder; Barrels; Roll of hog wire; Seed treater; Butter churn; Homart pressure system complete; 1 cream separator; Channel 6 T.V. antenna; Extension cords; .22 Cooey repeater; .12 gauge shotgun; Fire extinguisher; Quaker oil heater; Quantity of nuts and bolts; Steel stone skid; A large quantity of scrap iron; Monarch oil bath pump jack; A general run of farm tools.

SCHLENKER AUCTION SERVICE

AUCTIONEERS:
JIM SCHLENKER
Alta. & Sask. Bonded
Phone 527-7376, Medicine Hat
ALLEN SCHACHER
Alta. & Sask. Bonded

CLERK:
ED. A. SCHAUFELE
Office Phone 527-2814
Res. Phone 526-4464
CASHIER:
WAYNE SCHAUFELE

Auction Sale

Anna Fischer

Brown, MacLean, Wiedemann & Nelles
Barristers, Solicitors & Notaries

WILLIAM Z. BROWN, B.A., LL.B.
(also of Saskatchewan Bar)
DAVID J. MacLEAN, B.A., LL.B.
(also of Saskatchewan Bar)
ROY J. WIEDEMANN, B.A., LL.B.
ROBERT B. NELLES, B.Sc., LL.B.

TWX 610-825-4792
PHONE 527-3343
P.O. Box 548
525 Second Street S.E.
MEDICINE HAT, ALBERTA

December 15, 1969.

Pritchard, Medhurst, Lerner & Wilkins,
Barristers and Solicitors,
P. O. Box 100,
Medicine Hat, Alberta.

ATTENTION: MR. D. H. MEDHURST

Dear Sirs:

RE: Estate of Fred Fischer =
    Our File DJM

This is to advise you that we act on behalf of Mr. Jacob P. Fischer, the deceased's brother. Our understanding is that you represent the Estate.

This letter is to demand from the Estate the sum of $10907.63 which represents $4,000.00 plus interest less payments made, money advanced to the deceased by our client in July of 1949.

Yours very truly,

DAVID J. MacLEAN.

DJM/mjd.

P.S.: We are enclosing a photocopy of our calculation of the balance owing.

Letter from Lawyers office

Looking Back

J. Dusevic, M.D.,
Physician & Surgeon
Phone 628-3261 — P.O. Box 9
Leader, Sask.

March 16, 1970

Mrs. Anne Fisher,
1010 Balmoral St.
Medicine Hat, Alta.

Dear Mrs. Fisher,

    I reved your letter of March 15 th. Here is the diagnosis after autopsy on your late husband:
1. Carbon Monoxide poisoning,
2. Acute pulmonary congestion and edema,
3. Fatty Metamophois of liver,
4. Generalized arteriosclerosis, slight.

Result of blood examination:
1. A level of 0.11% w/v ethyl alsohol was found to be present in Exibit G(2), blood.
2. Exibit G(2), blood, was found to be 39.7% saturated with carbon monoxide.

                                    Yours sincerely,

                                    J. Dusevic, M.D.

The autopsy report from Fred's death.

Anna Fischer

The promissory note that Jack Fischer took to his lawyer to make a claim against the Estate of Fred Fischer. After original copies were requested for proof of authenticity, Jack Fischer dropped his claim to the Estate.

Looking Back

The Fischer Family: Dale, Fred, Audrey, Bruce, Anna (standing), Melinda

*After Fred's funeral my parents and brother Adolf
with his family came to the farm for a visit.
Back Row: Anna Fischer, Otaria Roth, Karl Roth, Melinda Fischer,
Lori Roth, Audrey Fischer, Gary Roth, Adolf Roth standing)
Front Row: Dale Fischer, Jeffrey Roth, Bruce Fischer*

Anna Fischer

*Our first Christmas after Fred's death.
Back Row: Bruce, Anna, Dale
Front Row: Melinda, Audrey*

*Lily & Elmer Mueller were our good neighbors at the farm.
They were a tremendous help after Fred passed away.
Elmer and Lily never asked for anything in return.*

Looking Back

My drapery business in the 1970's

After supper, father invited all to go up to the living room to talk more. I stayed back and helped with the dishes, we had many helping hands and didn't need mother's help. I told her to come with me upstairs so she could take part in the conversation. We were all sitting in our living room. The talks between Mrs. Fischer and my father continued. My father always was happy to have company. Mrs. Fischer was telling us that their parents came from the same area in Alexanderfeld. My father was saying that Alexanderfeld was only 35 km from our village of Johannestal. My dad was telling Mrs. Fischer that we had relatives in Alexanderfeld, by the name of Gribele. Anna Gribele was a cousin to my dad.

Mrs. Fischer started to talk of her family. She named her sons, starting with the youngest son. Carl was married to a Lutz girl, Alice. Henry is married to a Schafer girl, Sally, and they have one girl, Ivy. Andrew the oldest is married to an English women, Shirley, and they have three children. She said how the English people are a little different. Shirley wastes so much food, even with the three children. She told how the canning isn't good, as she doesn't even use garlic in her pickles. The talk went on and on. It didn't interest us in the least, as we didn't know them at that point. Mrs. Fischer failed to mention that there was no electricity, and no fridges to save food for a longer period of time. I wondered how Mrs. Fischer could speak to poorly of her daughter-in-laws.

Fred was sitting with my two brothers, Gottlieb and Adolf, joking and laughing and having fun. Finally the time came for Fred and his mother to be off to the farm. He jokingly announced that he might have to play midwife for his cows. His cows were just ready to calf at the time. Sometimes trouble would show up, especially with the yearlings. My two brothers were smiling, as this all sounded like fun. Fred and his mother were now leaving for the farm, and my family and I were tired from our busy day. All of us went to bed for the night to get rested for the next day of work.

Fred came to visit as often as he could; it was a busy time for him with calving time and getting equipment ready for seeding. On Fred's next visit, I asked Fred how his mother enjoyed the visit with my family. Fred said that his mother had a wonderful time meeting my family, talking about the olden days and times back from the old country. Then came the silence.

I had the feeling that Fred was holding back. Finally Fred said, "Anna, I will tell you what Mother was saying on the way home about you". I was told Fred that I had the feeling that there was more. Fred said that his mother said, "Fred, what do you want or see in her? She has no ass and no tits". Fred told her mother that he has to find somebody that like him too. Fred told me that he was so angry and mad at his mother. He told her that she'd never travel with him again.

I said to Fred that parents are always concerned about their children no matter how old they are, and she is still your mother. You are the one that is still with her, and she depends on you. Could it be that she is afraid that you'll find somebody, and afraid of losing you, and then she would be alone. Fred said to me, "Anna, you hit the nail on the head"! Fred never thought of it that way, but agreed that I was right. I reminded Fred that she was still his mother.

Time went and I was busy with work at the Glass Factory. Shift work was taking its toll on me, especially the midnight shift from 12 - 8 in the morning. When I started at the factory I weighed 139 lbs and in a short time I went down to 115 lbs. My body slowly adjusted to my schedule, and I started to regain some of my weight. Fred continued to come to Medicine Hat when time permitted, usually on my days off.

If Fred hadn't come to Medicine Hat in two weeks time, my parents and siblings asked if Fred was coming. It seemed that they missed seeing him. By Fred driving back and forth, it was taking too much time from his work. Fred came in on the weekend, and I told him that he should stay home and do his work. Fred replied, "Work on the farm is never ending". Fred said to my surprise, "what do you think, would you marry me"? I think we should get married he said. I said, "Fred we hardly know each other, it's just a short time". Fred told me that he met my parents and the rest of your family, and had nothing to criticize, and I came from a good family. I didn't give Fred an answer right immediately; I didn't know what to say. I was thinking to myself that we weren't even engaged yet, and to think of marriage. I thought that first you get engaged and then get married. I thought he is smarter to make sure I accepted before he spent his money on a ring. I told my family that Fred had proposed, and my father told me that it is up to me. I was an adult, and old enough to make my own decision.

In the meantime, my Uncle Wilhelm came in from the farm. My father mentioned to him of Fred's proposal. I just had stepped through the door when my Uncle jokingly said; "Anna I just heard the news that you are going to be a farmer". I caught on right away, and I told him that I wasn't so sure. I like my job and for the first time in my life I was making money to bring home to my parents. Uncle Wilhelm told me that I couldn't go wrong, as he knew of the Philip Fischer family, and they were good people. I was 27 years of age, and was my choice to stay an "old maid" or take the chance and get married.

I couldn't get the words "OLD MAID" out of my mind. Old maid was a term used in the early days when a woman never got married. It was often thought if a woman never married... something was wrong with her.

I felt deep in my heart that Fred was an honest man. Besides he could have kept back from me what his mother thought and said of me, but he chose to tell me. Two weeks again had passed, and Fred showed up like clockwork. Fred asked me if I had enough time to think about his proposal two weeks prior. I told him that it was a very hard decision to make for me because of the money I've been earning. I think you are an honest, and good man. So if you want an answer, I say, "Yes". Fred gave me a big hug. I had it all figured it out that he wanted to be sure that I accepted before he spends his hard earned money on a ring.

Fred asked me if I had time to go down town as he had business to do there. It was my cleaning day at home. He told me that I could clean later. It was a busy time at the farm, and he wanted to get back as soon as possible. We drove down town, and Fred was looking for a parking spot on the street. He told me that we were going to the jeweler store to see what they have.

As soon as we entered the jewelry store, the gentleman behind the counter brought two sets of engagements rings out from below the counter and set them on the counter in front of us. Fred asked, "Are we going to try on wedding rings"? The first thing I looked for was the price tags. We were taught by our parents never to buy the most expensive item. Sometimes the cheaper item looked better than the most expensive one. I tried on the cheaper set, and Fred requested to me that I try on the 2nd set. I picked out the cheaper set anyway. I still remember

Looking Back

the price for the set of rings was $98.00. Fred was asking me if I liked the ring set, and I replied, "*Ya*". Walking out of the store, Fred told me to keep the ring on. My English was still poor, even though I was already in Canada for 4 years. Before my job in the factory, I always worked with German immigrants like myself, and German was the language spoken at work. I understood more of the English language than I could speak.

Fred was saying that we would have to make one more stop at the men's clothing store. We entered Hawthorne's Men's Store, and the sales clerk brought a suit to Fred. Fred tried on the suit, and it looked dashing on him. To me it seemed that all was arranged at the jewelry store and the clothing store beforehand.

The sales clerk packed the suit in a suit bag, hung it to the side, and handed a slip of paper to Fred. Now our shopping was done, and we exited the store.

Fred said to me, "Now we're engaged". I looked up at him, and jokingly said to him, "Oh how romantic". I for sure knew now everything was planned before we had gone down town. Fred took me back home so I could continue with my cleaning, and he headed back to the farm, so I thought. Fred had gone back to the store before closing time to straighten out his bills.

I had found out later that he had purchased a small house for his mother to live in Medicine Hat. Fred's mother was not aware that she was going to move, and she was not counting on moving. It was not up to me. I suggested having Fred's mother to live on the farm with us. This idea was not acceptable to Fred. Fred had come to Medicine Hat several times, anxious to make down payments on the little house for his mother.

Fred's mother didn't want to leave the farm. I understood the feeling; it was her home, the place where she raised her children. Again I told Fred that it was ok for her to stay at the farm. I would have more time to help Fred on the field that way. Grandma Marie could stay in the house and do what she liked, even if she would only make supper, it would help, and would be good for her to be active.

Fred said to me, "Anna, you don't know my mother. It won't work. We found her a little house, where she can easily walk to her sister's place for a visit". There she would feel more at home. I felt sorry for Grandma Fischer; it was hard for her to give up her home. I again told Fred that I was sure that we could all get along; I was a quiet person and wouldn't interfere. Again it was not up to me, I had no say. It was Fred's mother not mine.

I remembered well the feeling and understood the feeling of having to give up our own home in the old country. I believe Grandma Fischer's heart was broken.

Fred had made all the arrangements for our wedding day and the reception following the ceremony. Fred planned everything because of my poor English. Fred had completed all the plans for our wedding. Our wedding day was booked and set for August 12, 1955, the same day as my birthday. My wedding dress was borrowed from my cousin Kaye Roth. Borrowed as well was my veil, and flowers. My bridesmaids were my sister Hilda, and a very good friend of mine, Tillie Pahl. The groomsmen were my cousin Emanuel Roth, and Fred's 2nd cousin Marvin Fischer. The wedding ceremony was held in the Evangelical Church on Allowance Avenue in Medicine Hat, with Pastor Riegel officiating. The reception was held at the Connaught Golf Course.

The Sunday morning after the wedding, after breakfast, we started to load my belongings on the truck. Along with me came my bedroom suite, living room suite and my kitchen table and six chairs. Before I got married my parents gave me permission to save up for my hope chest. My brother Adolf had built me a coffee table and two end tables for the living room. As well as other little side tables that I could arrange in the farmhouse.

Monday morning after breakfast, I asked Fred what needed to be done. The furniture was arranged, and farm life was a whole new experience. Fred had just the day before our wedding, baled

Looking Back

and stoked 21 acres of oats. Fred showed me how he wanted it done, and I was familiar with the work because I did it in the Ukraine. This is how we spent our honeymoon. I went on with my job, and by evening I had finished staking the 21 acres of oats. I walked back to the yard, and I was now going to do the daily chores. The cows were waiting beside the gate waiting for their chop, and ready to be milked. I took the milk back into the house, and went out again to feed the pigs. I went back into the house to separate the cream from the milk. The cats and dogs were given some milk as well.

Now I had to plan to make something for supper. Fred told me that he would be working until dark. Not familiar how to light up the mantel light, I discovered the kerosene lamp in one of the bedrooms. I lit it so I wouldn't have to sit in a dark room of the house. Now I wasn't too anxious to make supper, Fred would have to eat leftovers from the wedding.

Fred's mother was moved off the farm before I moved out to the farm. I wondered many times how she was doing. I never had the chance to even see her when she lived in Medicine Hat. It was harvest time and we didn't drive to Medicine Hat very often. We had no phone, electricity, or indoor plumbing on the farm. One day a man from one of our neighboring farms came and brought us a message. The man was Joe Tuchscherer; they had a phone in their home, and received the message that Fred's mother was in the hospital. Fred told me to get ready quickly; we were going to Medicine Hat to see his mother. We drove right to the hospital to see my mother-in-law. It was a nice surprise that a neighbor to my parents was in the same room as Fred's mother. Mrs. Klaudt was praising my family to Mrs. Fischer, and how Mrs. Klaudt and her husband visited with the Roth family often. I asked my mother-in-law how she was feeling. She replied to me that she was ok, and then she told me that she was sorry. I never asked any questions regarding her apology; there was no need. We returned back to the farm, and kept on with our work.

Anna Fischer

Two months later, we received word that Mrs. Fischer had passed away. Fred went to Medicine Hat with his brothers to make funeral arrangements for his mother.

I couldn't believe that the headstone from his father was stored in our attic, just waiting there for their mother's name to be added. Mr. Fischer died in 1950, and buried in the small country graveyard, only a couple of miles east of the Fischer homestead. The day before Mrs. Fischer's funeral, Mr. Fischer's remains were moved to the Hillside Cemetery in Medicine Hat so both parents would be laid to rest side by side. Mary Fischer's name was chiseled into the headstone and placed on the head of the gravesite.

I had the feeling that Mrs. Fischer after passing away only two months after Fred and I were married, she surely died of a broken heart.

From the time I set foot on the Fischer farm, I could feel the isolation, especially when night fell. I was homesick for my friends and family. I enjoyed the freedom of living on the farm. Even with my hard work, I still at times was overcome with loneliness. I enjoyed being around people. Many times I stood looking over the fields to the neighboring farms, wishing that I could befriend them to have company.

One day Fred was planning to drive to the store in Horsham, Saskatchewan to the post office to pick up the mail. We then dropped in at his brother Andrews farm on the way home. The visit was going to be a short one, as we were very busy at home. From the moment that I had met Shirley, Andrew's wife, I had the highest respect for my sister-in-law. I found that Shirley was a schoolteacher in 1940 before her marriage to Andrew.

I liked Shirley, and was pleased we got along well, I felt embarrassed that I couldn't correspond with her properly because of my poor English. I became a Canadian citizen after five years in Canada. I visited with Shirley and got to know her well, she was my favorite sister-in-law. She never bad-mouthed anyone, for I knew if someone badmouthed another in front of me, surely I was also bad mouthed behind my back.

I was warned from day one when I moved to the farm as to who to trust and who not to trust. I was raised by my parents to always be nice to people, and you would be treated kindly back. My mother taught me that if one has nothing nice to say, you better say nothing at all. I felt like I belonged to my new home on the prairies, and I never became bored. I could see the work that needed to be done everywhere I looked.

In the Ukraine, we never saw a rock on the nice flat fields, with dark, rich soil. On the prairies it was a different story. I discovered very quickly the picking-of-rocks on the fields were never ending. It was a huge disappointment to learn that the work of picking rocks would become a yearly chore. I became used to it, as the work was mindless. This was the only difference, but I didn't let the rock picking bother me. I felt so sure the rocks would end some day. I longed for the one day of rest... Sunday. I loved to go to church on Sunday morning in Hilda, AB just to see and be around people. I loved to socialize. This gave me the opportunity to invite friends or be invited. I didn't think that one day off during the week was not too much to ask for. Fred worked every day from early morning until the dark of the night.

Through the work habits of Fred, I adopted the same. I didn't want to be called the "Lazy Immigrant". I knew better not to let that happen. I made the remark to Fred, "If God would not have created night and day, would people ever stop working"? That was the reason that God created days for working and nights for rest. I had brought this jokingly to Fred.

No matter how much work I had in front of me, I still loved if somebody drove down the road to the yard. I was always happy to see people. In the beginning I suffered many lonely spells, and I longed to be with people. Not being able to drive was one big hindrance. It was quite common in the 1950's that women didn't drive. It was not so important or necessary for women to drive. The men did the driving. In reality, many women, including myself, would have been better off knowing how to drive. If I would have known how to drive, I would have been able to drive in the surrounding area, get together with neighbors; meet new people. I felt like I was losing out not being able to drive. I didn't expect to be as isolated on the farm as I was; I experienced too well the fear and isolation under the communist regime. Now I was living in a free country, and I loved the freedom in my new life. If I could drive, it would have helped Fred immensely. I could have helped Fred move machinery from one field to the next; then I would have had the opportunity to drop in on the neighbors.

One day our neighbor Elmer Mueller came to the yard to see Fred. I had asked this man who he was, so I could tell Fred who was calling. Elmer said to me, "Don't you recognize me"? I'm your neighbor and we were at your wedding". I felt so embarrassed, I had seen so many people on that day, it was difficult for me to remember the faces that were at the wedding. The only faces I remember were the faces of my family and my friends whom I missed dearly.

However, one of my sister-in-laws, never let me forger her face. She could drive, and with that she came driving their truck into our yard and visited me with her little girl. I became accustomed to her visiting. She spoke German, and she spoke A LOT! I so much wanted to belong in the community. I thought my sister-in-law was fun to have around, and especially because she spoke my language. My English was still very poor and I appreciated that somebody was visiting that I could communicate with. She often visited twice a week.

Even with my heavy load of work on the farm, I still made time for a visit. She always had lots to talk about. Many times she would tell me about the news of people in the surrounding area. It was not of any concern to me; I hadn't known the people of whom she spoke about. I sometimes have the feeling that she watched every movement I made. At times I became uncomfortable and nervous around her. It just so happened that my sisters gave me a bag of panty hose that had holes and runs in them. I wore them out in the stubble fields to avoid being scratched on my legs. My sister-n-law noticed me wearing the panty hose during the day to work. In those days, women never wore pants. Skirts and dresses were worn, and the women's legs would get scratched working out in the stubble field.

Before long, the rumors were circulating around the area. She said, "Oh, Oh, Fred can work till he hangs his tongue out. She wears panty hose out in the field". Fred had warned me of her, and replied, "See I told you so". I didn't take Fred seriously; I thought it was that Fred just disliked her. We found that more was to follow. I knew better, I was brought up in poverty, and I knew how to save the pennies.

I took all this gossip with a grain of salt, as I had too much work do than to worry about what the gossipers were saying. I found little spare time besides baking, cooking and all the outside chores. I continued making time for the visits from my sister-in-law and her little girl. She had many questions. Some of her questions were too personal for me to justify an answer. On one visit, my sister-in-law said to me, "Anna, *gell* (right), everybody has sex before marriage". I looked at her and thought; what is she fishing for? I told her that I could not speak for everybody or anybody, but your remark is all too personal and is nobody's business. I was wondering what she was fishing for.

Fred had arrived that day from the field nearby. After sitting at the table ready to eat, with a grin on his face, he said he noticed that I had company today. I told him his favorite sister-in-law was here along with her little girl. He asked, "What did she know today"?

Jokingly I said to Fred, our sister-in-law wanted to know if we had sex before marriage. Fred said to me, "are you kidding me"?

I told him that I was not joking with him. And what else is she coming up with. You see I told you so and I'm warning you that there'll be more to come. Fred sounded angry. Fred declared that our sister-in-law lost a few marbles up stairs. She didn't realize that by her question, she had given herself away. The five-cent brain didn't quite reach that far. By her own remarks, she didn't realize that she had given herself away.

Fred said the brainless remarks will never stop nor will they end. This is what she was very good at. I couldn't believe it, and there it was proven, Fred was right.

After two years of marriage, and our family had begun, soon the remarks were heard that one could smell that there were babies in the house. Our gossipy sister-in-law remarked how I was sitting like an old hen with her chicks around. The gossip was circulating in the area, and the gossip came back to us. Fred was upset to hear the continuing gossip, he was angry, and said how her elevator didn't reach the top. I told Fred to let it be, and if people don't know any better, we have to accept them as they are. Fred was upset, but he avoided the friction that his sister-in-law was creating, so he kept his mouth shut.

Yes, in fact I was very busy with my children, and they were born very close. My baby Bruce was not yet two years old, and our second son Dale Wesley was born, than when Dale was eleven months old, my twin girls were born, Audrey Marie and Melinda Ann. There were diapers and more diapers every day with four babies in the house. For three years, everyday there was a five-gallon pail full of dirty diapers soaking in bleach water. I washed the diapers during the night when the babies were in bed. Fred told me again that the gossip wouldn't stop. Our sister-in-law was very good with her words. At times I was hurt by what she said, but I kept on doing the work that was in front of me.

Forty years after my husbands passing, at the funeral of our nephew's wife Margaret Fischer on August 30, 2010. It was a very sad day. My two daughters and I attended the funeral at St. Paul's Lutheran Church in Medicine Hat. After the viewing of Margaret in her casket, we moved over the side. We noticed my sister-in-law coming through the door; she looked around to see whom she knew. She noticed the three of us standing. She came toward us, and stretched out her hand to shake hands with my two girls. She then shook hands with me, replying, "Oh we haven't seen each other for so long, but you look so shriveled up in your face". It was more than thirty-five years since we had seen each other, and found it quite inappropriate to her odd greeting. I could hear in my mind Fred saying to me, "I told you so, it'll never end". So I came face to face with my sister-in-law, and realized that some things never change. She had never changed in all those years.

At the beginning of the days on the Fischer Farm, for the longest time I couldn't help wondering and thinking, what is it in the Fischer Family. To me it seemed that there was a wall between the brothers. The families were not close like mine were. They lived so close to one another, but so far apart. I could not feel closeness in their family. It struck my mind about what Fred had said to me about his mother. "You don't know my mother", he said. This sounded so unusual to speak of your own mother this way. One whole family of Fred's brother did not attend our wedding, as I knew there were five brothers and one sister in his family. I thought in time I would find out. I had a feeling there was a line that ran both ways between the one brother and the rest. I simply couldn't understand this kind of life. I soon had noticed the Fischer family was not raised with a motherly love, such as giving children praise, a hug or a kiss for a job well done. There was no time in the Fischer family for bonding; there was only work, work and more work. I could see when Fred had mentioned to me that his mother had a birth or a miscarriage right on the header box in the field.

If you don't receive you cannot give, and this is what lacked with the Fischer brothers.

Brotherly Love

A while after I had found out the real story behind the Fischer brother feud.

As the story unfolded among the brothers; when their father, Philip Fischer was alive, he needed help with financial matters. He took with him his oldest son Jack. Jack went along with his father whenever Philip was to purchase any implements, parts or pay for repairs. This was only done when the cash was available. Most of the time, they went to the small hamlet of Hilda, Alberta. Philip needed to inquire about some piece of machinery, so as usual Jack went along with his father. When the deal was done, Philip paid cash and Jack signed the document. I was told Philip couldn't read nor write, so Jack wrote for him. Philip though didn't realize that Jack was writing his name on the bill of sale instead of his father's name. Jack was married and had his own place and was farming on his own.

Philip had problems with his health, dealing with Asthma and breathing problems. He became ill, and passed away in 1950. Andrew, Clara and Henry were married, and the youngest brothers Fred and Carl still lived at home with their parents. Clara and Jack had a double wedding. Brother and sister married brother and sister from a different family. Clara Fischer married Edwin

Looking Back

Gomke and Jack Fischer married Hulda Gomke in 1939. Shortly after Philip's funeral, Jack came to the Fischer homestead and started to load up equipment and parts. These were the things that he had signed for his father. On paper it showed that Jack owned all the equipment and the rest of his brothers now owned nothing. Fred jumped on the truck and started to throw things off the truck while Jack was driving down the road. Jack started to speed up, and Fred continued to throw items off the truck that landed in the ditch.

From then on the rest of the brothers had to work together to purchase the necessary equipment for farming and work together. Loans needed to be paid off for the equipment that was bought.

Andrew and Henry by now had their own homestead established in the surrounding area. The brothers were still working together during seeding and harvesting time until they were able to afford each their own equipment and go on their own. The four brothers were now completely disassociated with their brother Jack.

At the same token, Jack didn't acknowledge his own mother. He would say in public that Mary Fischer was not his mother. Some people told him, "Jack, you always can be sure of your mother, but you can never be sure of your father". Jack didn't fancy the reply. It was his father that Jack had cheated his brothers, Jack's own flesh and blood. It was so sad to hear things like this went on within family. Life is too short for so much hatred and greed. Jack took advantage of his own father who was illiterate, and his father had trusted Jack.

I myself could not believe this all took place. My cousin Martha Bechtold and her husband was the neighboring farm to Jack. They never had anything to do with each other, as Jack never socialized with anybody. To her surprise Jack one day paid a visit to the Bechtold farm. Jack asked them if it was so that his brother Fred was seeing a cousin of Martha's. Martha said,

"Yes, and she'll make a good farmer's wife". Jack told Martha that she should tell her cousin not to marry Fred. Jack said that Fred was a no good bastard, and will not make a good husband for that girl. When I heard this, I thought to myself, what kind of mess am I getting myself into? Jack was speaking so badly about his brother. After that, I believed what Fred had told me, and everything became clear to me. I could never believe that it could be possible that your own brothers, sister and mother, their own flesh and blood were parted in this way forever. After our marriage and 14 years on the Fischer homestead, it became the homestead of Fred Fischer.

The Fischer brothers never associated with each other very much. It was hard for me to understand. I believe it was due to the way they were brought up. I missed the togetherness of my family. I missed my parents and my siblings. They were always there for me when I needed help. I was always happy to see them when they came for a visit. My family was very close to each other.

Fred was amazed how close our family was. At one time he made the remark that we couldn't leave mother's breast. It bothered me when he said that. The Fischer brothers, when they were together would laugh with each other about others. This upset me. I told him that I never ever wanted to hear this in my home, especially around the children and when my family was at the farm for a visit. To my surprise, I was pleased that the gossip had quit around our home.

This behavior had stemmed from their upbringing. They had "nicknames" for everyone in the surrounding area. I was happy to see this come to an end.

The games were even played on me. Fred one day told me that he tested me to see if I was a big spender. I said that I had a feeling that he was up to something. Fred gave me some money and at the end of the day he wanted to see how much I had left. In other words, Fred wanted the perfect wife who did not spend money foolishly, did not smoke, did not drink, and knew how to clean, and one that works like a horse.

Fred had found what he was looking for, and he was satisfied. He told me so.

We both turned out to be "workaholics". I never regretted having to work hard, as it made Fred happy.

Now being in Canada for 5 years, I became a Canadian Citizen. I was very proud of my citizenship papers. It gave me the feeling of being able to belong to Canada, which was now my country, the country of freedom. I could see the pride in my parents and the rest of my siblings after being sworn in as Canadian citizens. For the first time in our lives we felt like we belonged. My father was standing so tall and proud holding his citizenship paper.

A year after I was married, my brother Gottlieb got married. The next following year, my brother Adolf was married. It seemed that for the next few years there were nothing but weddings in the family. All that was left at my parents' home were my four sisters, Hilda, Kay, Rose and Helen. My youngest sister Helen was close to the age where she could go to work and help the family financially.

Fred and I were working hard to build a future for our family living on the farm, the same as his parents and grandparents. Now looking back on my life on the farm, there was no time for rest. It amazes me what a person can do when you are young. The motto is so true, "if there is a will, there is a way". I had enough will power to do what was in front of me and if you love what you are doing, work doesn't seem like work. We worked hard, it seemed like we were born to work.

I had the feeling that I wasn't able to share my past during the war with Fred. I didn't think he would understand what I had been through, as he never experienced the same hardships as I had gone through. Yes, everyone was poor all over the world during the war, but he wasn't taken from his home. He wasn't raised under pressure and fear.

Anna Fischer

Fred was born in Canada, in a free country, the complete opposite from my life. None of my relatives from Canada really realized what we went through during the war. People wanted to know so much about back home. They wanted to know what it was like living through the war and enduring hunger after describing the horror. One of my cousins popped up and declared, "Why were you so dumb? You should have taken a gun and shot the bastards". When I heard that, I thought it was better for me to keep silent, they didn't understand. I kept everything inside of me.

Our life on the farm had continued with hard work. I was happy the German language was in the Fischer family, as well as some of the surrounding neighbors spoke German. I found later the people were very down to earth. Everybody was living the same way; all had no money and survived on the land.

Fred and I became proud parents of our first-born baby boy, Bruce Frederick, born January 1st, 1957. Fred was so proud of his little farmer, but it turned out our little Bruce was born with the same symptom of hay fever, asthma and allergies. It was very hard with many visits to the pediatrician, Dr. Brooks. It seemed all those doctor visits didn't help; we walked the floor nightly. Bruce was constantly crying; we tried everything to comfort him. Bruce often went into convulsions, which scared us terribly. I also didn't have much sleep myself. I was expecting our second child, and still no further ahead with the problems we were having with Bruce's health.

One night Bruce developed a fever, so in the morning we decided to take Bruce to see Dr. Brooks. It just so happened that Dr. Brooks was not at the emergency room in the hospital in Medicine Hat. Dr. Skinner was on duty for that day. Dr. Skinner was Medicine Hat's coroner. We had no other choice but for Dr. Skinner to treat Bruce. Once we were taken to Dr. Skinner's office, I started to explain Bruce's symptoms. Dr. Skinner sitting in his chair, reached for a big, heavy book. I figured that he was looking up the symptoms in his medical book to find out what could be done to help Bruce.

Dr. Skinner ordered some blood work to be done, and gave us some medication and some ointment to rub on Bruce's arms and legs. Bruce was scratching himself until the blood ran.

We were returning back home to Saskatchewan, but both of us had little confidence that Bruce was going to get better. Just as all the other appointments turned out with Dr. Brooks. When we got back home, Fred went to do the chores and I was preparing the baby for bed. I fed him his bottle of milk and the medication given from Dr. Skinner, and rubbed the ointment on his tiny arms and legs.

By now, after the long day, we were ready for bed. We once again were prepared for another sleepless night. Before I went to bed, I looked in Bruce's crib, and he was lying there so peaceful sleeping. We were so tired from the endless nights of walking the floor with Bruce. Fred and I both fell asleep, and when we woke up, the bright sun was up. A shock came over me, and I said to Fred, "oh the baby". I ran over to the crib, and to my delight, Bruce was looking up at me with a smile. We couldn't believe what happened. Whatever the Doctor had given for Bruce had worked. For the first time in a year, we had a full nights sleep.

The sores on Bruce's arms and legs were beginning to heal. In a week time we were to bring Bruce back to see Dr. Skinner. When we got to the Dr., he told us that the baby was very low on red blood cells to the point of being anemic. We were to keep up with the medication, and the baby would be all right. And so it was, but he still struggled with his allergies and hay fever. We soon found out not only was he allergic to dust, and pollen; he was also allergic to fish. We were so thankful to Dr. Skinner for helping make our little baby well.

On November 26th, 1958, our second child was born. We named the boy Dale Wesley. We were so thankful that he was a very good baby. He just ate and slept, and Bruce was getting better day-by-day. Dale, on the most part slept during the nights. Fred was convinced that Bruce would grow out of his allergies, as he got older. Now with two babies, Bruce at twenty-two months, and Dale a newborn, I thought I had my hands full. I had two babies and the chores outside; on top of all that all the household duties.

I had no automatic washing machine. Electricity services were starting to be installed in the rural area. I used a gas operated wash machine, and I had no drier. The clothes were hung out on the wash line to dry. I did my work during the nights, especially washing the diapers. Diapers were hanging all over the house to dry. The best time to wash diapers was when the babies were asleep in their cribs. By daybreak I had bread in the oven baking.

By October 9th, 1959, we had added to our family,

A set of twins were born, two girls, Audrey Marie and Melinda Ann. Now I had four small babies along with all my chores and housework.

Audrey was born a very sick baby. She was born with clubbed-feet and choked every time she was fed. The Doctors in the hospital had given up on her. She needed lots of time, especially at feeding time. Melinda was released from the hospital, but Audrey had to stay. Audrey had to be fed every two hours, even throughout the night. Every time the nurses at the hospital started to give Audrey her bottle of prescription formula, she started to choke. She couldn't get her air, and after two weeks she was released and we got to take her home to the country. On feeding her though, she was continuing to choke. We were not aware of her problem when we brought her home.

At feeling time I was so afraid to give Audrey her bottle, that I asked Fred to help me. The girls' pediatrician, Dr. Hook was telling us that Audrey would grow out of her choking episodes. The girls reached two years of age, and Audrey still had her choking problems when she ate and drank. One time Audrey found a way to help herself with her problem of getting food caught in her throat. She put her little fingers down her throat, forcing herself to gag and throw up. This made the food that was stuck and bring it up.

With the age of just over one year of age, Audrey's little legs were put in casts and braced to begin the process of straightening her legs. By this time Melinda was holding on the table and walking. It was so sad to see Audrey's face, watching her twin sister walking. Audrey began to cry, she wanted to walk too, and she wanted to do what her sister was doing. A few days later, Audrey got brave and was trying to lift herself by hanging onto the table. She watched Melinda's every move. Audrey with her casts and braces began to walk, copying every move what Melinda made. There was no stopping little Audrey, she was walking around everywhere she could grab hold onto something for support. When Audrey turned two and a half years of age, she needed to start wearing orthopedic shoes that were fitted to her feet. As her feet grew, she needed new fitted shoes. The shoes made such an improvement in straightening Audrey's feet, although her ankles remained weak. Audrey needed to wear her orthopedic shoes to school to protect her ankles. The doctor told her that she wasn't to partake in any sport activities in school like running and jumping. It was a complete NO, NO. But she did, one couldn't expect a child not to run, and play, as this is just normal for a child. Audrey was jealous of her sister, as Melinda got to wear the pretty shoes and Audrey had to wear the orthopedic boots. In time her ankles became stronger.

Fred very rarely found time to visit neighbors and friends. I considered myself lucky; my parents and Adolf and his family came to the farm often on weekends to visit. Fred liked Adolf's company, and Adolf was always willing to help around the farm. The cousins all played together and had fun roaming the farm, climbing in the trees, and playing in the fields. My brother

Anna Fischer

Adolf was a carpenter by trade, and was the foreman with the Construction Company he was working for.

Adolf kept busy when he was at the farm. He helped build a garage where Fred kept the car and ½ ton truck. Graineries and a summer kitchen were built which I used as a butcher house. I was grateful for Adolf's work at the farm. Fred gained the knowledge from Adolf on how to construct buildings the proper way. Fred told Adolf that he had learned a great deal about construction.

I was extremely excited that Adolf had built me my cupboards for the kitchen. There were no cupboards in the kitchen when I first came to live at the farm. Adolf's wife, Margaret was busy helping me with my chores at the farm as well. She was especially fond of the heavy sweet cream, cheese and fresh butter. Margaret had a passion for baking. She baked her favorite German Torte'. I was happy to supply the dairy products; this was a small price to pay for all the help they both provided.

Adolf and Margaret had three children and we had our four. When they all played together, the farm air filled with liveliness. We were all happy to hear the laughter of them playing together. Margaret stayed busy making lunch for the kids. I am still to this day very thankful for my brother Adolf and my sister-in-law Margaret and their generosity and help. Adolf will always be my special No. 1 brother.

Adolf worked for Johnson Construction, but his boss Mr. Johnson's health was failing and his business had to close. Adolf purchased some equipment from Mr. Johnson, and in the early 1960's Adolf had started his own construction business. At that time A. Roth Construction was born.

Fred mentioned to Adolf of his own health problems with asthma, hay fever, especially when in the dust. Adolf was busy building homes in Medicine Hat, and Adolf suggested to Fred that he move to Medicine Hat and work with him in the construction business. Fred was considering to possibly semi retire and make the move. He figured he could work for Adolf in

Looking Back

winter and in the spring, do the seeding and in fall the harvest thinking that maybe his breathing problems would improve.

At the time we were seriously thinking of building a metal Quonset. We had a large red wooden Quonset, but Fred would like a building to store his machinery.

Fred was trying to make a decision on what to do. He saw opportunity in front of him. Many times Fred mentioned that he was waiting for the right time to make his decision to move to Medicine Hat and work for Adolf. Fred seemed to be excited at the time.

I was concerned about Fred's health. Fred never went to see a doctor for his condition. Fred symptoms of running nose, asthma, and hay fever sounded like the same symptoms that his father had. There were more than a dozen handkerchiefs, red and blue with white polka dots in the washing machine each washday. Mentioning to Fred to see a doctor was like talking to a stone wall. Fred always replied, "What can they do"? Fred was aware that he had the same health problems like his father did. Fred should have never been a farmer with his health problem.

When we went to Medicine Hat, I looked forward to seeing my parents, and hoping that they might have had any news or some kind of information about our loved ones or others that were missing. I never lost hope that someday we would receive messages from our people from the handful that had survived through the ordeal out of Siberia's torture.

Ten years after WWII had ended, Dr. Adenaur, a German government official, was invited to a meeting in Russia with Kruschev. Thanks to the German councilor, Dr. Adenaur had brought up the fate of the German people in captivity and also the prisoners of war.

After the meeting it still took time before the "commentadure" was removed. Also Dr. Adenaur was discussing with Nikita Kruschev to release the German prisoners to return to Germany to their homeland. Slowly the people in captivity were feeling their freedom. They were allowed to travel in there surrounding areas but were not permitted to travel to the once called home place in the Ukraine. They were allowed to go to Asia. It was the time we were hearing that many were moving to Alma, Ata in Asia where the weather was warmer. Russia started slowly beginning to release prisoners of war to return home to what was left and survived the torture in Siberia.

The people were allowed to start to get in touch and start corresponding with the Western Countries and other countries. Messages were being heard that people were coming out of slavery with the help and the continuous searching through the Red Cross. The search continued for our missing loved ones.

After the long years of waiting, finally we received a message. Full of excitement we received our first message from my father's youngest brother's wife.

My Aunt Hulda wrote:

Heinrich was drafted into the German Army without training. He never had a gun in his hands before. As the Russians had reached close to the Polish boarder, all the German people were ordered to flee toward the west. The farmers that had taken children and I in, supplied us a small wagon and one horse. I was bundling up the children; set them each on the wagon back to back with their feet hanging over the wagon edge. It was bitter cold of January 1945. There was no room on the small wagon. I walked beside the horse leading him. I was also expecting our 8th child. By having the children hang their legs off the wagon, 3 of the children had badly frozen their feet. The 2 children from Heinrich's first marriage were taken away during their flight, and my own little one also was the one that had frozen her feet. I didn't want to give her up for I feared that I wouldn't see my youngest again.

I crossed the German border with the rest of my children. In the Northern part of Germany again, we were taken in by a German farmer. Heinrich had been wounded and was released from the hospital. Through the Red Cross he was able to relocate and joined us.

Looking Back

Two days later the Russians crossed the border and in the middle of the night, we were taken away. Heinrich was taken from us to work for the Russians, and for the rest of us, we were taken across the border into the barracks in Poland.

In the beginning of winter in 1946, along with thousands of others, were deported to Siberia. Through this all I lost my newborn baby of 6 months old. Baby Helmut was left behind and buried in the woods. When we arrived to our destination in Siberia, Lena (oldest daughter) and I were forced to work laying trees in the forest. Martha (2nd oldest daughter) was only 14 years old, and was forced to work on the railroad tracks with other 14 year old children. Through the heavy lifting that Martha had to do, she sustained internal injuries and died. Heinrich was released from the Russians, and through the Red Cross he located his family. He joined us in Siberia. He was sick and very weak, and there was little to eat. Henry was to hunger driven. Heinrich asked Lena to take him to the city market spot (Bassar) to see if he could get food by begging. On the way it was very icy and Heinrich fell and received internal injuries and he too passed away.

Heinrich and his daughter Martha are resting side by side under a tree in Siberia. His own family dug the graves. I am still working, and every morning the call came "Dawy-Dawy to Robota" (Come out, come out to work). I was ordered to work on the railway track the same as Martha.

Later on Hulda wrote that she was still working on the track, pushing heavy wheel burrows day after day. It was very had work, and getting so little to eat. She was forced to work in the Trud Army and if the quota is not filled, the food rations were cut. All that is left is to struggle and hope every day we would be able to fill the quota to get the little extra for the hungry children at home.

Our next exciting message was received from my father's sister's daughter, Rosa. Rosa wrote:

Anna Fischer

Uncle Karl, we were so happy to receive your address through the Red Cross. It is sad that I have to inform you that my mother and father passed away in 1947. They both starved to death, times were bad. The starving and dead people were carried out daily from the barracks.

Now Uncle Karl, the burden is on me. I have to be parent to my 14-year-old brother Rudolf and my 10-year-old sister, Bertha. We are living in terrible times. We are constantly hungry.

As much as we miss our parents, we have to say my mom and dad now have peace. Their suffering has ended. No more hunger and no more cold.

The only thing, which is hard to take, is that they had to stave and be buried in the Siberian wilderness. My brother Rudolf and I with the help from some good people, we dug our parent's graves. We laid our parents to rest under a tree and said good-bye. Mom and Dad rest in peace.

For me it was sad to hear of their suffering. I was familiar and knew what it meant. The hardships from my own people were heartbreaking. We all had experienced the misery, poverty and hunger.

My heart went out for them, but we were helpless. Even when we send something to them, they never would receive the packages. We kept sending packages, and finally they let us know not to ship anymore. In later years we were able to send packages again, but the duty was very high.

The first years of our marriage, things were tough. Some years the crop was not so good, and the price of wheat was low. We operated a mixed farming operation. We grew grain and raised cattle, pigs, chickens and ducks that helped.

Fred always was striving to get more land. With luck, we were able to add two more quarters of land to what we already had. Now Fred was content with owning seven quarters. It was enough land for the size of equipment that we had. Fred was proud of his farm.

Looking Back

Fred was proud of his two boys; they were daddy's boys. He also was proud of his twin girls, Audrey and Melinda. They were always the babies. Fred was a proud father of his four children.

In the 60's, Fred bought a Quonset. He was fond of his machinery and being able to store his equipment indoors over the winter. Fred said that we now had our farmers to inherit and keep on farming when the time came for us to retire.

For me my work never was ending from morning till dark. We worked for our four children's future. I was busy with my housework, after the children returned home from school. Supper had to be ready after the children's homework was done. My work continued even after the children went to bed sometimes after midnight.

Fred and I were hoping that the time would come when we would get help from the children around the farm. This would give us more time to visit with friends and relatives. I loved to be around people.

Death of a Husband and Father

On the morning of November 22, 1969, we got ready to drive to Medicine Hat to take Audrey and Melinda for their piano lessons. Mrs. Andreas was their music teacher. After dropping the girls to do their lessons, we planned to get some groceries from the Co-op grocery store. After the grocery shopping was done, it was time to pick up the twins from their piano lessons. Usually we went to my parents for supper after the girls had their lessons. We arrived at my parents' house we all got out of the car. But Fred said he was going for a quick drink at a bar, and would be back soon.

Time was passing and we were all waiting for Fred to return so we could eat. We decided to eat and Fred could to eat when he returned.

The children were getting tired and were looking out the window and waiting for their dad. They were hoping that he would come soon.

I mentioned to my parents that I maybe should phone him. My father was telling me not to worry, that he was surely to come;

Looking Back

he's not a child. It was close to 11:00 pm and Fred was still not back. The children were very tired by this time and the girls fell asleep on the couch. Finally around midnight, the boys spotted lights approaching down the street. Fred pulled up to the side of the curb in front of the house. It seemed odd that he pulled up to the house with the car parked facing the wrong way. The children were glad that their dad finally came back. They started to run out of the house and toward the car. Bruce, the eldest of the children, was the first one to the car. Fred told Bruce to sit in the middle in the front seat of the car just in case Bruce needed to drive. Bruce was only 12 years old, had no license to drive, but drove the vehicles on the farm.

As I entered the car I was wondering why Bruce was sitting in the front, but I thought that it would allow the other children more room in the back seat. I closed the door to the car, and I suddenly could smell the strong smell of alcohol. Fred was wearing his amber colored sunglasses. I didn't know that Fred was intoxicated when I entered the vehicle, and that is why Fred asked Bruce to sit beside him so Bruce could let him know when his dad was driving on the wrong side of the road. All four of the windows on the 1968 Ford Galaxie were open. Fred started to drive and I noticed Fred needed the whole street to drive. He was driving on the left side, then on the right side of the road. Then swerving to the left and to the right again, over and over. At times we was driving toward oncoming vehicles. At first I thought Fred was playing a joke on me, but I realized very quickly that something was terribly wrong.

I told Fred to stay on his side of the road. He tried to say something, but only mumbling sounds came from his lips. I wasn't able to make out what he had said. It seemed as though his tongue was impaired. I started to panic. A terrible fear came over me, for a moment I thought of jumping out of the car. I couldn't, I couldn't leave my children alone, in danger. I thought if we must die; I'll die along with my children. Fred drove very slowly. Bruce sat beside Fred, every now and then telling his father to stay on the right side of the road. I was very scared. Huge vehicles were on the road. Bruce once again, was reminding his dad to stay on the right side of the road. It seemed like a lifetime until we reached Highway 41. Fred continued driving on the wrong side of the road, entering the lane of oncoming traffic. Everyone in the vehicle sat quiet as mice; huddled together trying to stay warm, not knowing if we would make it home.

Nothing needed to be said to the children, it was understood that they needed to be quiet. They knew something was not right. At one point I told Fred to get on the right side of the road, and he got angry with me. I had to trust Bruce to do the coaching, as I silently sat praying for our lives. I believed that night we all would be killed. I truly believe that we had a guardian angel looking after us.

By the time we hit the Schuler turn off, I felt somewhat relieved that we were no longer on the highway. It was a gravel road, and I thought that if I needed to get help, there were several homesteads that I could walk to.

As we approached the hamlet of Schuler, the whole town was dark and silent. We had another nine miles to go until we reached home. It was our saving grace that Fred drove slowly. Those nine extra miles seemed like eternity.

Finally we entered the approach to our farm. Usually a forty-five minute drive, turned into a two-hour nightmare.

Fred backed the car up to the steps so the groceries could be unloaded. I told the girls to go to bed while Bruce and Dale helped me with the groceries. I put the groceries away and Fred drove on over toward the garage.

The yard light had the yard lit up. Bruce and Dale were on their knees looking out of the living room window. Focusing towards the garage watching their dad. Bruce said that his dad had driven into the garage and was walking outside beside the garage. Bruce said, "Mom, look dad is walking funny. He's

Looking Back

walking from one side to the other". I told the boys to go to bed, that their father would probably be in soon.

Now all the children were in bed. Fred still had not come to the house. I felt sorry for my children that they had to witness their father in the state that he was in. I was in disbelief that something like this was happening. In all the fourteen years of marriage to Fred, I had never seen him intoxicated. I'm sure that Fred never wanted his children to see their father this way either.

Fred couldn't take much alcohol with his allergies and asthma. I remember Fred having a bottle of beer last in the fridge for a week at a time. I often questioned him as to why he would drink such stale beer. Surely by now it had no more taste. His reply was always the same, "it still makes wet".

As the children lay sleeping in their beds, I was thinking how grateful I was that we were safe at home. I left the lights on in the house and kept the yard light on for Fred. I was still waiting for Fred to come in the house and go to bed. I lay down on top of the bed fully clothed. I was exhausted and fell asleep. I don't remember how long I slept, but I suddenly woke up panic stricken as if a knife went through me. Fred still hadn't come into the house.

I darted off the bed, looked out toward the garage and saw that the garage door was closed. I heard a loud muffled sound coming from outside. In panic I screamed out to Bruce, "Bruce come, dad is still outside, something must be wrong". Bruce was out of bed like a bolt of lightning. We both ran out of the house toward the garage. The doors were closed. We opened the side passage door to the garage. The garage was full of smoke exhaust.

The car was idling inside the garage. Bruce quickly opened the driver side door of the car. He reached for the key and turned the engine off. I reached in to help Fred. I wasn't able to move him; he was unconscious. I cried, "Oh my God, I can't move him".

His lifeless body lay on the front seat. He gasped his last few short breaths. I said, "Oh my God Bruce, go for help". We had no telephone on the farm. Bruce took his bicycle and started to ride the one-mile drive to Henry Fischer's farm (this was Fred's brother). Bruce didn't know that his father had taken his last breath when the car door was opened. It was the middle of winter, and I can't even imagine the determination that came from Bruce that night.

When Bruce arrived at his Uncle Henry's farmyard all was dark. Bruce pounded furiously on the door for someone to answer. Henry opened the door, and there to his surprise was Bruce. Bruce told Henry that he needed to come, we needed help, something was wrong with dad. Henry got dressed, and rolled himself a cigarette. If Henry would have known how serious the situation was, I'm sure he would have hurried. Fred sometimes had been taken to the Emergency department on account of having water in his knee, and Henry no doubt thought that this was again one of those times.

I was waiting for what seemed like a lifetime. I started crying, trying to comfort the children who were also crying. I was worried that something happened to Bruce because he was gone for a long time. I thought he perhaps he fell off his bike on the way to Henry and Sally's farm. I saw light coming down the road. It was Henry with Bruce in the passenger side, the bike on the back of the truck.

As Henry stepped out of his truck, I stood on the steps crying. I sobbingly told Henry that something was wrong with Fred; he's in the garage. Bruce and I had opened all the garage doors before Bruce rode off for Henry's help. Henry went into the garage; only seconds after Henry came out of the garage.

I will never forget the words Henry said to me, "Oh shit, *der isch jo tot* (Oh Shit! He is dead)". I was in shock. I walked in and out of the house, sobbing. I didn't know what to do. Bruce, Dale and the girls were all crying. I was in denial of what Henry told me. The way Henry uttered those words were so unfeeling, so uncaring, and so callous.

Looking Back

Henry got into his truck and was heading to his brother Andrew's farm. Andrew had a phone that he could use to call the police.

The police and Dr. Dusevick, the coroner from Leader, SK were contacted. My 4 children and I were alone on the farm, just waiting for help to arrive. We were all in tears. I just couldn't bring myself to enter the garage. I was so frightened, so unbelieving of the truth. I was praying that this was not real, and I would wake up any moment and all would be just a bad nightmare.

Daylight approached, and I hadn't realized how cold it was. The temperature was just above the freezing point. It was nearing the end of November, very cold, but there was no snow yet. I was walking back and forth from one bedroom to the other watching over my children. I was hoping soon some help would come for Fred. I just couldn't get the words out of my head, "he's dead". I was hoping Henry was wrong, I was hoping for a miracle. People make mistakes all the time. This couldn't be happening.

The wee daylight hours were here. I heard the sound of vehicles coming down the road toward the house. I saw a police car and the coroner's vehicle. The police and coroner entered the garage and I prayed with everything I had, "Please God, don't let them say dead".

The police officer and the coroner entered the house. The children were in their beds, Audrey and Melinda were crying under the sheets....hearts broken ....their dad was gone. Bruce got out of bed and told me that he hadn't slept all night. Bruce and Dale were both in such anguish. The shock and pain...unbearable!

The police took Bruce into the living room for questioning because he had been beside his dad while driving; and at the same time I was questioned in the kitchen. By now word had gotten out and people were coming to the yard. I was in shock. I noticed the Bechtold's had arrived as well as my cousin Ben Roth from Burstall, Saskatchewan. I couldn't think or feel; I was

Anna Fischer

numb with shock, frightened for my children, frightened for myself. I lost Fred...he was gone! How could of such a horrible accident happened?

The moment came when the hearse arrived; my heart was aching, the crying, and the tears. My cousin Ben, talked to the funeral attendants from Cook's Funeral Home and helped lift Fred's lifeless body into the hearse.

Later that morning Martha and Henry Bechtold took my four children and I to Medicine Hat to my parents' house. Audrey remembered how her grandfather, Carl was sobbing when we entered my parent's home. My dad thought the world of Fred. We stayed at my parent's house while the funeral arrangements were made. Cook's Funeral Home was in charge of the funeral, and the service was held at St. Peter's Church in Medicine Hat. Fred's funeral service was held November 25, 1969. This was the most dreaded day of our lives. Dale's birthday was November 26, the day after the funeral. Just can't imagine how he felt inside, grieving for his father on his birthday. He turned 11 years old that Nov 26/1969.

Today I still struggle and try to understand how this could have happened. Fred was such a careful, meticulous person. Many times the question came up as to how my husband died from other people. Sometimes the odd person would ask if Fred took his own life. I believe that in the state he was in that dreadful night, he was cold and didn't realize he was in a closed building and started the vehicle to get warm. Fred had a habit of resting in the car often when we went to Medicine Hat. Many times after lunch you could find Fred having a nap in his truck or out on the field taking a rest. The fumes filled the garage that night and took his precious life.

Fred had so much ambition. We worked very hard to build up our family life. Fred had so many plans and looked forward to it. In hindsight, so many things crossed my mind, and how I would have done things differently. I am so sure that Fred would have never wanted to leave his family behind without seeing his children grow up.

The day after the funeral was Dale's birthday on November 26. My brother Adolf and his wife Margaret came to my parent's home where we were staying. They had brought a little gift for Dale otherwise it would have been forgotten. No body was thinking about birthdays and birthday cakes. The following day Adolf took us back to the farm. My parents were willing to come with us and stay on the farm.

There were cattle to be fed, cows to milk, and the children were just starting to write their exams. Dale, Melinda and Audrey attended Horsham School and Bruce attended Richmound School.

Now I had lots of responsibility in front of me. I was hoping to be able to keep the cattle, and wanted to sell the cattle in the coming New Year. I remembered that Fred said that our income for the year was high, and he was planning to sell the cattle after the New Year. The New Year was only 5 weeks away. I planned to stay with my children on the farm until the cattle were sold. I was determined to do what needed to be done with the help of my two little boys, Bruce 13 and Dale 11.

I leaned toward Henry (Fred's brother) to keep an eye on things for us. I so desperately needed help. I asked Henry if he would be so kind and keep an eye over us if needed. I also asked Henry if he would like to rent our land, and Henry flatly refused to everything. He blurted out that he had enough on his own. I was willing to let the Fischer brothers have the first chance to rent Fred's land, but all refused.

I strongly believe looking back that the Fischer brothers had a different agenda. They had forgotten that Fred had left 4 little children behind. There was no regard for my children and myself. I couldn't believe at the time that they could be so cruel and refuse to help us. Usually it is family, your own people; that one leans on in a crisis. Now I was forced to make arrangements to sell the cattle in December. None of the Fischer brothers volunteered to help me look after the cattle. The cattle were loaded, transported to Medicine Hat and sold at auction.

The moment Fred passed away, the trouble started brewing. Fred's brothers were scheming as to how they could get Fred's land in their possession. They believed that because our farm was the Fischer home place, their original birthplace, the land was rightfully theirs. They didn't want to see that a woman from Germany would be left with the farm. They had no regard of the four children left behind.

Elmer Mueller, our neighboring farmer helped us in our time of need. He helped load the cattle and transport them to Medicine Hat. Without the help Elmer and Lily Mueller I don't know what we would have done. Elmer and Elva Bertch were also there for us. I was so grateful that these wonderful people stood by our side and still remain friends.

Andrew, my brother-in-law took all of Fred's papers and went through everything. He was looking for a copy of Fred's will. Andrew asked if I knew where there were more papers. We searched through all our kitchen drawers, but we couldn't find anything. I told Andrew that Fred had only one spot for his papers and he had whatever there was.

Fred didn't have a Will. We had to see that we got a lawyer for Fred's estate. I appointed Andrew as the administrator for the estate and I understood that Andrew needed all the documents. Andrew desperately searched for a Will. I wondered how many young men thought of making a Will in the 1960's.

My parents stayed with my children on the farm while they still went to the country school. The children stayed just until they received their report cards just before Christmas. Andrew and his wife Shirley came in the morning to pick me up to go to the lawyer appointment. My lawyer was Mr. Medhurst. He was very good at his job, and was working hard for my children and I. Mr. Medhurst jotted notes of all the information regarding

Looking Back

the estate. As Andrew was my administrator, the lawyer took Andrew's phone number as to keep in touch for the upcoming appointments. I had no phone on the farm so this seemed like the most logical thing to do besides you should be able to trust your family.

On the farm we had two large fuel tanks that could hold 500 gallons each. Both tanks were filled with purple gas, usually used for farm machinery. In the garage was a barrel with regular gas used only for the new 1968 Ford Galaxie 500. Fred was so proud of his car. Don Anhorn was the local gas agent who came to fill the tanks with fuel. Fred filled these tanks every fall so he could use the expense on his taxes. It was a way of balancing the income with the expenses.

My parents were a great help to stay with the children and myself on the farm after Fred's funeral. We were planning to get more details settled and then going to move to Medicine Hat. I didn't know how to drive, and we didn't have a telephone, so I felt very isolated. If pipes would freeze or if someone would get sick I would be stuck with no way of contacting anyone.

After the funeral, Andrew came to the yard almost every day. Each time he would fill his vehicle with the fuel that Fred had filled in the tanks. Andrew said that he was going to take the fuel, as it probably would have gotten stolen anyway. I said nothing, but I was uncomfortable with the remarks. Locks could have been put on the tanks so the fuel couldn't get stolen. I should have said something, but I was very vulnerable at the time. I didn't want to make waves, and I depended on him to do the right thing.

By the 2nd or 3rd appointment with the lawyer, Andrew started to push for selling the farm machinery and implements. Fred at the time had some of the newest equipment around. All the equipment was in good condition. Fred was very meticulous when it came to how he kept his machinery and his workshop. Andrew continued to fill his vehicle from our tanks whenever he

Anna Fischer

came to the yard. He even came to the yard with his 3-ton truck and filled it up.

On the 3rd or 4th appointment with Mr. Medhurst, Andrew picked me up to go to Medicine Hat. Again Andrew was pushing to sell the farm machinery. Mr. Medhurst's reply was the same as before, "only if it is the best for the children and Mrs. Fischer".

Each time we went to Medicine Hat, Andrew filled up his vehicle with Fred's gas.

The cattle had been sold and were waiting for the cheque to arrive. The correct PO address in Horsham, SK was given, and could not figure out why the cheque was taking so long. Unbeknownst to us, Jack Fischer (Fred's brother), went to the livestock auction office in Medicine Hat and told the secretary to send the Fred Fischer estate cheque to Hilda, AB. Jack had taken the cheque to his lawyer's office and put in a claim against the estate at the office of David J. MacLean and Wiedemann.

We received a call from Mr. Medhurst to come and see him at his office. On arrival at his office we were told that the cattle cheque for the Estate of Fred Fischer had a claim against it. I was in shock and I started to cry. How could this be happening? How could Fred's own brother be doing this to Fred's children?

According to Jack Fischer's claim, in the year 1949, Fred had supposedly borrowed $4000.00 from Jack with a 6% interest rate. A per diem rate of $1.78 was even indicated. All the Fischer brothers protested. They had told the lawyer that Fred had never borrowed many from Jack. If Fred needed money he could have very easily borrowed the money from the bank for a rate of 2%. And at the time, Fred was still living with his parents and his younger brother Carl. I was very thankful to the Fischer brothers for standing by my side with the issue.

Andrew had made the remark that if Jack had borrowed that kind of money to Fred, and to wait to bring it forward after 20 years, just didn't make sense. Jack had no contact with any of his brothers in all the years since their father passed away. I was speechless; I wondered what would be next. Mr. Medhurst told that he would demand the original documents that Jack Fischer had in his possession to have it analyzed for fraud if this continues. It seemed so coincidental that the amount that Jack wanted from the estate was almost to the penny of what my cattle cheque was. Jack's was asking exactly $10909.63, which included interest and period payments over the twenty-year span. The amount of the cheque for the cattle sale was $12,000.00. Andrew knew Jack was not smart enough to fabricate the document by himself, and surely someone else must have helped Jack. Someone who was familiar with numbers, someone possibly who knew how interest rates worked. Shortly after Jack must have known he would be in serious trouble and he aborted his claim.

On our next appointment with the lawyer, again Andrew filled fuel with Fred's gas. Again Andrew said, "I think it is time to start thinking to sell some of the machinery". Andrew was well aware that we have to have an auction sale in the spring. Andrew was pushing for me to sell the machinery to the Fischer brothers.

Fred kept all his machinery in immaculate condition. And the Fischer brothers wanted it all. Andrew told me that the implements should be sold while we had buyers. Andrew said Henry will buy our new ½ ton with the new cattle rack, Andrew would buy something and maybe Carl would buy something as well. Lloyd, a nephew, would buy the fairly new harrows. I listened, but kept quiet. Andrew was waiting for the go ahead from the lawyer and me.

I couldn't understand why Andrew was being so pushy. Preparations had to be made to make a farm auction sale in the spring. What would be left to make an auction sale if all the best items were bought privately from the Fischer brothers, and at their prices, which were ridiculously low?

I wondered if there was pressure put on Andrew from his brother Henry. I believe that Andrew couldn't make all of these decisions by himself. I knew he must have had help. And all the while Mr. Medhurst had told Andrew that sell, only if it is good for Mrs. Fischer and her children.

Andrew kept on saying to me that if Henry buys the new ½ ton truck, we would leave the cattle rack with the truck. And if it gets sold to somebody else, sell the cattle rack separately. I thought, what does that tell me.

This didn't seem that this was in the best interest for my children, or myself. It sounded better for Andrew and his brothers. Did they not realize that they were taking from Fred's four children? Had they so little regard for these children whom had just lost their father. Their whole world was turned upside down. They were taken off their home, went from a small country school to a city school, so many strange and unfamiliar surroundings on top dealing with the grief and loss of their dad.

Andrew informed me that the gas that was in Fred's fuel tanks were now coming to an end, and from now on, he would be keeping track of the lawyer appointments, his time, the expense for gas, wear and tear on his vehicle, and all will be charged to Fred's estate. I was sitting and listening. Panic overshadowed me. How was I to pay for this all? I was worried that the expenses would be put toward the land and the land would be taken away from us.

It was now time for my parents to go back home as they had appointments they had to attend.

My sister's husband, Maurice Burkart was working in the hamlet of Hilda, and he agreed to stay with me at the farm. Maurice was a mechanic at Staub's Garage. He would commute back and forth from the farm to Hilda. It was only nine miles one way; it was closer than driving back and forth to Medicine Hat everyday.

Going, Going, Sold

My neighbor Elmer Mueller came to pay us a visit to see how we were doing. My father helped me set up saw horses and sheets of plywood to make tables to display Fred's small tools for the auction sale. The tables were set up in the red Quonset where a variety of small tools were placed on the tables which consisted of an assortment of welding tools, motors, drills, hand-tools, down to nuts and bolts.

    My father went to visit the outhouse; we had no indoor facilities. The door on the outhouse had small holes, so one could easily look through them. Andrew had arrived at the farm, and parked right in front of the red Quonset door. My dad could see right through the holes of the outhouse door to Andrew's truck window. Andrew was going in and out repeatedly, opening his truck door and closing it again and again. My father came into the house and told me what he saw from the outhouse. I went into my girl's bedroom, and I could see right through the window to Andrew's truck. The same repetitive, opening and closing of the truck door. My dad told me to go over and see what he was doing. I didn't know what to do. Dad told me that I needed to find something to say. I walked over to the Quonset. The walk seemed miles away. I entered the side door of the

Quonset. Andrew was inside. I asked Andrew what he thought of the setup of tables with the small tools on top. In case the weather wasn't nice on the auction day, it was nice to have these items under a roof. I told Andrew that I had every tool written down on a piece of paper to hand to the auctioneer. I wanted to make sure none of the tools grew legs. My dad came into the Quonset and began to strike a conversation, he too was curious as to what was going on. But he knew what was happening.

One Saturday morning Andrew came to the house and asked if my twin girls would like to go along with him and play with their cousin Velma. The girls really didn't like to go; there was not much desire to spend time away from home. I told the girls to go along and play for a few hours, and their Uncle would bring them back later in the day. My mother said she could see that the girls would have rather stayed at home, but we agreed. Perhaps getting out would do them some good. Bruce and Dale were entertaining their grandpa at home.

Melinda told me much later on in years that she had heard a very disturbing discussion while at her cousin's place. Melinda said when we got to the farm; Velma had spread out on the kitchen floor a jigsaw puzzle. Velma, Melinda and Audrey started playing on the floor with the puzzle, and in a short time, Velma's father Andrew came in the house. Entering the kitchen, with Henry and his nephew Lloyd Fischer in tow, they were deep in conversation. Andrew made the comment, "What do you think? Did she have something to do with it?" Lloyd replied back, "I don't thing so". Then Henry piped up, "I think she did it". They were implying that I had killed my own husband. Melinda had told me that they were talking about me. Audrey on the other hand was quite involved in puzzling, and didn't give the conversation at hand much thought. Melinda was playing, but was also listening, remembering word for word what was being said. To the end Andrew said, "We'll find out". When I heard this, I was for sure concerned as to what they were planning to do against me. Melinda didn't want to tell me right away, she didn't want to hurt me, and that is why she never disclosed what she had heard.

The Fischer brothers were so determined to have Fred's land, their father's homestead. But they didn't realize that this was the home of my four children and I. Now that Fred was gone, they were concerned that the land was now going to somebody from over there, I was that somebody from over there. I think that my brother-in-laws feared that an outsider would farm the farm. I was 42 years old when Fred died, and they never had no consideration what I was going through, nor did they ever think how this all was affecting the four children. They were hurt devastated over losing their father. They forgot that Fred's 4 children carried the Fischer name as well.

Still on the farm, I was constantly worried if one of us would become ill. I had no phone and I couldn't drive. We stayed until the Christmas holidays started and the kids were out of school. We moved in with my parents after Christmas. Before moving I asked Clara if she wanted the pump organ back that she gave to the girls to play on. She told me to take it for the girls.

My parent's house was a small, two bedroom home. Bruce and I slept in the spare bedroom. Dale, Audrey and Melinda slept on the living room floor with all the flowers and wreaths from the funeral. The three children would take turns sleeping closest to the wreaths. Years later, did I first learn that they were petrified of sleeping next to the flowers and wreaths that were place on the floor from the casket. Night after night it felt like you were sleeping beside the coffin, having to relive the memory over and over again.

Andrew had made several trips to see Dr. Dusevic in Leader, SK. He was determined to get a hold of the autopsy report regarding Fred's death. Dr. Dusevic informed Andrew that as soon as the report was finished, the report would be mailed out. Andrew wanted desperately to find out if there was any foul play in Fred's death. I'm sure Andrew was hoping to find some kind of evidence stating this.

Elmer Mueller was helping me, and the Fischer's did not like the idea of the help Elmer was giving. Elmer helped load and transport the cattle to the auction, and now he was helping load up my furniture for the move to Medicine Hat.

Andrew had all the keys to all of the farm buildings, as well as the house. Andrew at this point was still the administrator of the Estate. Funny though I received no offers to help move from any of the Fischer brothers.

Elmer came with his 3-ton truck, and the loading began. Andrew earlier had suggested to me to leave the furniture behind. I didn't like the idea, and decided to move everything and store it into my parent's garage. I decided to keep Fred's car as well. Bruce in a couple of years would be old enough to drive when he had his driver's license. We could travel back and forth to the farm.

I gave Andrew the address and phone number of my parents place. I notified Mr. Medhurst's office where I could be reached in case something came up. It didn't take long, in less than a week the phone rang. It was Mr. Medhurst's office. The secretary told me that I had an appointment for 2pm.

I had lost over 40 pounds just walking in a daze and as I walked toward the lawyer's office, my sister-in-law, Clara Gomke (Fred's sister) came walking toward me. Clara asked where I was going. I told her that I had a lawyer appointment in the afternoon. Clara told me to meet her at the Woolworth's Store. She would be waiting there for me after my appointment. Walking toward the lawyer's office, I was thinking that Andrew would be there as well. I was afraid to see my lawyer alone. I was very self-conscious because of my poor English.

I was sitting in the office, waiting to be called in. I still couldn't see Andrew. I was called in the office. Mr. Medhurst started talking of business immediately. Your brother-in-law Andrew

Fischer is trying hard to sell the machinery, and apparently has several buyers in mind. I would like to know how you feel about this Mrs. Fischer. Deep in my heart I new my lawyer was searching for an answer before the next visit with both Andrew and myself. I told Mr. Medhurst that I knew of Andrew's buyers, they were only the Fischer brothers. They were offering what they would like to pay. I expressed my concern over the fact that if the biggest and best machinery were sold off the yard, what would be left for an auction sale. All that would be left would be the little stuff. I didn't think the rest would bring out enough buyers to the auction to get the best possible price. I felt to auction off everything, and if the Fischer brothers wanted to purchase a piece of machinery, they could bid just like everyone else. That way they couldn't say they over paid.

Mr. Medhurst thought that what I had just said made a lot of sense. What will we do Mrs. Fischer? Here Mrs. Fischer sign these papers. I signed them. Mrs. Fischer, you are now the administrator of the Estate of Fred Fischer, your husband's estate. I was shocked and broke down crying. How Mr. Medhurst, can I do this? My English is poor. I have no English schooling and kept on crying.

You can do it all. All you need is your accountant and your lawyer, and this is what you have, and we're here to do the work for you. I had appointed Andrew Fischer as the administrator for the estate. Andrew was asked to be administrator, verbally only. Nothing was ever signed. Mrs. Fischer, now you need to go out to the farm and inform Andrew that you have taken over as administrator of the estate. Pick up all your papers and keys. Lock up all the buildings, and prepare for your auction sale for the spring.

After leaving the lawyer office, as promised I walked toward Woolworth's to meet Clara. As I entered the store, Clara and her husband Edwin were standing waiting for me. I apologized for taking longer than expected. There were a few clients before me, and the wait time was longer.

Clara started right away speaking in German. "*Was fur eine sauerei*" (What a mess), over and over. "All the people are talking". Clara, what is it, what are you referring to "that" mess. What are the people talking about? I didn't care what people were talking, people always talk. Clara told me that I shouldn't have gotten married to Fred and he shouldn't have gotten married to you, then this mess wouldn't be. Clara, what are you saying? What do you want from me? Clara, is it the land? "*Ya*, then everything would be on mother's name; then it would be ours". Did Clara stop to think of what she was saying?

Had Clara expected Fred to stay single? So the land would stay on the mother's name. After all, their mother had passed away fourteen years earlier. It was such a brainless remark. Surely Fred would have found someone if we hadn't gotten married. Clara you aren't thinking of your deceased brother and his four small children that Fred left behind. I feel very sorry for you, and turned and walked away with tears swelling in my eyes. Clara and I parted ways for ten years.

Now I concentrated on preparing the farm for the auction sale. I was able to get a ride to the farm. I worked on preparing as much as possible and in the evening I stayed overnight at the neighbors Elmer and Lily Mueller. I asked Elmer if it would be possible to drive me to Henry Fischer's farm to pick up the smaller pieces of tools and belonged to Fred. By entering Henry and Sally's house, I told Henry that I asked Elmer to bring me here and I was there to pick up Fred's tools. The Fischer brothers were still aiming to get their hands on Fred's equipment. Suddenly out of the blue Henry exclaimed that there is talk. People are asking if they were not man enough to get the land in their hands. I told Henry that I had offered them to rent the land, which they all refused. You told me you had enough of your own. Can you not remember that?

Henry why are you saying this? The land belonged to Fred, and now it's for Fred's four children. Henry with his 5 cent brain, as Fred would have called it, told me that they would say that I "did it`". Henry had just accused me of harming my own husband. They threatened to take the four children and the land and I would be in jail. I was shocked. Henry do you think the police and the coroner's office were dumber than you? I would not even have been able to be at my husband's funeral. I grabbed the tools and Elmer, Lily and I walked out of Henry's house. I was hurt and crying. Elmer and Lily were in disbelief as to what they had just heard with their own ears.

Driving back to Mueller's farm, I was thinking to myself; will they ever understand and quit with the accusations, and realize that Fred's death was accidental. I stayed overnight at Elmer and Lily's house. It was clear to me that I needed to see what the Fischer brothers were after. I felt sorry for Elmer and Lily; they were being dragged in the middle. The Fischer brothers didn't like that Elmer was helping me. I was so thankful for the help of Elmer and Lily. With Elmer living in the same community as the Fishers, if something would happen that he would need help, where would he go? Elmer was just being a Good Samaritan who was helping someone in need. And I needed all the help I could get. I appreciated all the help I received. Elmer had never once asked for something in return. I was then and still am thankful from the bottom of my heart to Elmer and Lily Mueller for being such good hearted, kind people.

I was picked up to return to my children in Medicine Hat at my parents' home. The kids were glad to see their mom come home. I had the feeling my children needed me more than ever; I was now mom and dad to them.

It just so happened that my brother-in-law Carl Fischer, my husband's youngest brother, lived in Medicine Hat. They had moved a year prior to Fred's death. Carl needed to drive out to the farm that he had sold in Saskatchewan, and I asked if it would be possible to catch a ride to Andrew's farm to pick up my papers and keys as my lawyer had instructed me to do.

Carl had business to do, which didn't take too long. Then we arrived on Andrew's farm. I was to inform Andrew in a gentle way that I was now the executor. I explained to him that spring was approaching, seeding needed to be done and a busy time for any farmer. I told him that I was taking over the administrative position for Fred's estate, that way he wouldn't have to waste time going back and forth to Medicine Hat for appointments. The news took Andrew by surprise. He was speechless, in shock I guess. Now that I was living in Medicine Hat it would just be easier and cost the estate less for fees. Because Fred had no Will, all bank accounts were frozen, and I didn't even have money to purchase groceries.

Mr. Medhurst and I went to the Bank of Montreal where we did all of our banking, and released fifty dollars so I was able to pay for the children's school supplies. I was told to keep track and document everything that I had purchased. Fifty dollars didn't go very far. I was lucky that my parents provided and shelter for my children and myself. We lived with my parents for eight months.

I could see Andrew didn't like being cut off of the job as administrator. Andrew was still determined to find out what had happened to Fred. I know all the Fischer brothers wanted to know what was in the autopsy report. I was glad that Carl, the youngest of Fred's brothers gave me good advice when I needed it. I knew I could trust Carl. Carl and I were sitting in Andrew's home for more than two hours. Two hours of waiting for Andrew to release our papers and keys. I saw Andrew was hesitating on releasing the documents and keys. I turned to Carl and said, "I think we better hit back to Medicine Hat. If Andrew doesn't release the papers and keys, then he'll have to take them to my lawyer". Finally Andrew went into his room and brought out a box of papers. I took the box from Andrew, and asked about the keys.

Andrew told me that he would meet us at my farm. So Carl and I drove to my farm. On the way I asked Carl if he had an idea what Andrew was up to. Carl didn't know what was going on, but something not good. I felt sorry for Carl as he was now being dragged in the middle between his brothers and me. In the meantime, Andrew went with his 3-ton to his Brother Henry's farm. Both brothers came in each of their 3-ton trucks to my farm. Henry and Andrew opened the red Quonset and the steel Quonset. They started loading their trucks with the fanning mill with all the screening, several large cattle troughs, wheel barrels and much more. I kept quiet while they were loading. Andrew told me that these were in share with all the brothers, and were not of much value. I was thinking, if the things they were loading up were of no value, why then were Fred's two brothers loading up to take it away. I couldn't find the words to say. I was lucky that I had Carl on my side that day. Carl got my attention, and motioned with his head, for me not to say anything.

Walking into the house, Andrew was going to take the fire extinguisher. Carl gave me the sign with the blink of his eyes and the expression on his face; which meant NO! I said to Andrew that the fire extinguisher was going into auction and he could purchase it then. Andrew was going to take Fred's 22 rifle, again watching Carl's movement, he gave me the sign. I again refused Andrew, and said it will be sold at the auction sale.

After Andrew and Henry had their trucks loaded, Andrew handed me the keys. Carl helped me lock up the buildings, and we were ready to head back to Medicine Hat. On our way back I asked Carl if he knew of any equipment shares between the brothers. Carl never knew of any, nor any shares in any of the items that his two brothers had loaded on their trucks. I broke down and cried. I thanked Carl for being with me for the day. I don't know how I would have handled things had I been alone.

Anna Fischer

Carl was a great help to me, and the most honest of all of Fred's brothers. Fred and Carl were the youngest in the family and the closest to each other. Tears streamed down Carl's cheeks while he was driving. I could see his heart was breaking. Carl told me how his brothers always belittled him, as if he was nothing more than a piece of dirt under a pair of old shoes. Carl and Fred were close, and Carl looked up to Fred when he needed help. Carl's right hand was now gone. Carl in a crackling voice told me that in a short time he would be hearing from his two brothers. They would be accusing him of being on my side, but I told him that he had done nothing wrong. Fred would have been thankful and happy that I could depend on you at this time of need. On arrival in Medicine Hat my children were always happy to see me back.

A short while later I received a letter with all the items that they had taken, and the prices that they said they paid. They tried to make it look legal and the list read paid out shares to the Estate of Fred Fischer.

I couldn't think of a single reason to why we were so badly treated by the Fischer brothers and Fred's sister. We were family; at least I thought we were.

I received a call from Mr. McPhail, he was the insurance agent for an insurance policy Fred had. Mr. McPhail needed to see me. I knew of a small insurance policy that Fred had with our two sons, but I had completely forgotten about it. It didn't amount to much. I was sitting in Mr. McPhail's office and asked for his advice. Who would be entitled to get my husbands results from the autopsy and the death certificate? Would it be for me, or would it be for the brothers of my deceased husband? In a moment Mr. McPhail had Dr. Dusivic on the phone. He handed me the receiver and told me to find out for myself. I told Dr. Dusivic who my husband was, and asked, "Who was first inline to receive the results for my deceased husband. Was it for Fred's children and myself or Fred's brothers? I'm so glad you called Mrs. Fischer. Definitely it will be you and your children. As soon as it arrives on my desk, I will send it directly to you. Please be patient as this all takes time. Andrew was in the office quite often enquiring for the results. I thanked Dr. Dusivic and hung up the phone.

A few days later Andrew was in the Horsham General Store, and overheard Elmer Bertsch saying that he had to go to Leader to do some business. Andrew asked if he could catch a ride there. Elmer said he had enough room for a passenger.

When they got to Leader, Andrew immediately headed for Dr. Dusevic's office. Dr. Dusevic informed Andrew that he will not receive any results of the deceased's death, and the deceased's family will be getting it. Andrew was not expecting what he had heard. On the way back, Andrew never mentioned the conversation that he had with Dr. Dusevic. Andrew was very quiet on the way back. Elmer dropped Andrew off at his farm. Elmer, how much for the ride? Nothing, I had to go there anyway. Just charge the gas to the Estate of Fred Fischer, Andrew told Elmer. What did Andrew mean? The trip to Leader had nothing to do with Fred's estate. It made Elmer angry.

I got to hear of this story at a later date when I stayed on their farm over night. One could plainly see that the Fischer clan was up to no good. I believe they wanted harm to come my way, and they would take the children just to get ownership of Fred's land. Elmer Bertsch offered to help me arrange the machinery on the farm for the auction. I knew I could not depend on the Fischer's for any kind of help, nor was I offered any help from any of them.

One day Andrew came to Medicine Hat to pay me a visit. Along with him was the Lutheran Minister from the Lutheran church in Hilda, AB where we all had been members. Andrew and Pastor Score came to my parents home, all were polite, but I was wondering for what reason they had come. Pastor Score told me that the reason we came here today is that Andrew would like to stay in good terms with you and your children.

He would like to continue being an uncle to the children, and a brother-in-law to you.

Both of you should mend your disagreement. I thought for the children's sake, I was ready to go the distance, and keep the peace. One never forgets the wrong, but one can forgive. I reached my hand out to Andrew. Andrew I will say sorry if I wronged you, if you can do the same and say sorry to me. We can apologize to each other, and we can continue as family. "I have nothing to say sorry for, I have done nothing wrong", said Andrew. I looked at Andrew in shock. I turned to Pastor Score, and looked at him in silence. What did you people come for, I said to Pastor Score? He had no answer, Pastor Score just stood there, with his head looking down at the floor.

As Andrew and Pastor Score were leaving the house, Andrew turned facing me, pointing his finger at me. "I have to find out how Fred died even if it costs me my land", Andrew shouted at me. I stood in disbelief. I couldn't believe the hatred and greed I had just witnessed. Looking back, every one of the Fischer brothers are all gone now, taking their hatred with them to their graves, just because they could not bring themselves to say sorry.

I received help setting up for the auction sale from Elmer Mueller, Elmer Bertsch and cousins of Fred's. Everything was now in order, everything clean and ready for auction. The day that I dreaded, seeing everything being sold off to the highest bidder. People coming for the ultimate deal, and for me, was heartbreaking to see the farm the Fred loved, being strewn with people coming to take it away. All that would be left was the shell of the farm, the heart taken out.

April 8, 1970 had quickly arrived, the day of the auction. Jim Schlenker from Schlenker Auction did the auctioneering one piece at a time. "Sold" was heard over and over. Ed Schaufele, my accountant from Schaufele's Accounting was there to document all the sales. This was required because there was no Will made, and all the documentation was to go to my lawyer.

Looking Back

August and Martha Fischer from Hilda had arrived early that morning to offer their help. August was Fred's cousin, as well and very good friends of ours. We had many visits back and forth together. They stayed very good friends to me to the end of their lives. After Martha's death, August frequented my house for a good home cooked meal, company and went home again. The children remember him coming quite frequently, and enjoyed having anyone that belonged to their dad around...family.

That same morning Emil and Beula Ehnis from Burstall also arrived to give their help in any way. Martha and Beula went to the summer kitchen and got a big pot of coffee brewing. Sandwiches were being put together for people to eat. I wasn't much help that day and I truly appreciated all the help that I received. I was too stunned at what was going on. I brought water from the well to the summer kitchen for the coffee. I would cry the whole time as I was fetching water.

I was trying to hold on in my mind to everything that was. Life was not going to be the same. Now the machinery and farm equipment started selling piece by piece, it was hard to take. Fred and I had worked so hard to build up what we had for years. It took only a few hours to have it gone.

So many rumors were flying around amongst the onlookers at the auction. The Fischer brothers were standing together, just watching. They were hoping that the auction sale wouldn't bring as much money as what they had wanted to pay me. They bought not one single item, but before hand they had tried get it cheap from me. I had laid my trust in God's hands. Whatever happens, let it be. Elmer Mueller and Elmer Bertsch helped move items on the table as it was being sold.

My sister-in-law walked several times in and out of the summer kitchen. She was talking to Martha. "We were going to buy the new ½ ton with the cattle racks", Sally said. "We offered her 800 dollars, and she didn't take it. "She won't get that, it won't bring that much money", Sally sounded sure of herself.

Anna Fischer

If it brings less, then it will be so much better for you to buy it, or you would have overpaid according to your offer", Martha answered her. Martha spoke her mind.

"SOLD", the auctioneer said in a loud voice. The ½ truck had been sold to the highest bidder for $1,200. The new cattle rack brought another $200.00 more. Martha inside the summer kitchen was so happy to hear the truck sold for even more than the offer from the Fischer brothers. Sally immediately left the summer kitchen, not showing her face to the ladies in the summer kitchen for the rest of the day.

I wasn't aware of the conversation that Sally and Martha had until later when the sale was almost over.

"Anna", Martha said." I was praying all through the sale that Sally would be wrong", Martha spoke silently.

As I continued carrying water to the summer kitchen, a man approached me. "Mrs. Fischer, I can see what you people had built up, it took years, and is destroyed in one day", he said sympathetically. I broke down and cried. The gentleman took my hand and wished me for all the best.

I had the door open to the house and noticed that many people had been going in and out. What for, I didn't know. There was nothing to see, the house stood empty without furniture. All that was left was the stove and fridge.

Another man came to me, "Mrs. Fischer, we seen with our own eyes, it is not what people are talking". He told me of the false gossip that was circling among the nearby communities. Talk was that I had wall-to-wall carpet, and us Germans from over there come to this country and then we want everything. It was rumored that I got what I wanted. Then it came clear to me what this man was speaking of. I was raised in a manner that if one had nothing nice to say, it was better to say nothing at all. My parents had instilled in all of my siblings good morals and values.

Looking Back

Martha and Beula stayed until the last item sold. The small items got sold first, then the biggest machinery and implements to last. This practice is common; as this way buyers will stay until the last item was sold to get the best possible price.

I cannot put down in words how I hurt that day. I felt like somebody was ripping my heart out of my body. I felt like dying. I thought of my four children. My poor little children, they were the ones that kept me going.

By evening the farmyard was empty. I stood looking across the yard where implements and machinery had once stood. It now seemed so barren. I mustered up the strength to pick up the wind strewn paper cups and napkins. Elmer Mueller was coming back to the farm in the evening to pick me up to go to their farm for supper.

The same day of the auction sale, Clara drove to Medicine Hat to my parent's home. She knew that I would be at the farm during the auction sale. Clara had loaded the old treadle organ onto their truck. She turned to my girls and said, "You're mom has lots of money now, she can buy you one".

The girls were taking music lessons from Mrs. Andreas. The organ belonged to Clara before Fred and I got married. Clara told me that I should take it. The girls could continue with their music lessons in Medicine Hat.

The old organ was on the Fischer Farm house already when we got married and moved in. Fred told me that the organ was bought at an auction sale, and was meant for Clara. Clara was the only girl in the family. Carl showed interest in the old piece and was playing by melodies by ear. When Clara got married, she no longer wanted the organ. So there it stood in it place on the farm.

As Melinda and Audrey grew a bit older, they showed some interest in the old organ. Starting to dibble and dabble on the ivory keys. They would sit for hours plunking away at the keys. The girls started with music lessons with a local girl, Janet Elle from Horsham as their first music instructor. Later their instructor was Mrs. Ollie Andreas from Medicine Hat. The girls had to quit taking piano lessons because the organ was taken away from them. It was such a shame that Clara took out her anger and hatred on her little nieces, Fred's two girls. The girls now hoped that Clara got good use of the organ that she had taken away from my two girls.

Many years later, one of my nephews came to me and said, "Aunt Ann, we know you were treated badly after Uncle Fred passed away. We heard and saw many things that were going on". Lloyd Fischer came to my drapery business, which was quite a surprise to me. It was during a time when he had troubles of his own. He was at the time renting an apartment suite in Medicine Hat. Lloyd had confessed to me that after Fred's death, Fred's family wrongly treated us. I asked Lloyd if he recalled the conversation that day at Andrew's house. Lloyd had remembered the discussion quite clearly. What did you think when Andrew asked you if I had anything to do with Fred's death? Lloyd had said that he told them that he didn't think that I had done it. He remembered the three little cousins playing on the floor while Andrew, Henry, and himself were in the kitchen. He also remembered Henry saying that, "I think she did it". Andrew replied that they would find out what happened. Lloyd admitted that the whole conversation between the three of them should have never happened.

Today I am saying thank you to all of you that came forward and told me the truth and still had respect enough for me to call me your Aunt. It made me feel good to be called Aunt Ann.

The saddest part was that after Fred's passing; my children were excluded from the whole Fischer Family. It was like we didn't even exist. There were no Xmas cards, no birthdays remembered. Even as their older cousins were getting married, my children were excluded from any such events. They also carried the Fischer surname.

Looking Back

It's over forty years since the passing of Fred. The farm still to this day stands proud. The buildings that are still there have been well maintained, and when a passerby would drive by, the yard looks like it is alive with somebody still living there. It sits there and waits for the many weekend trips made there. I am proud of my children, after all these years, they still hold the farm close to their hearts.

That evening when I came home from the shop after Lloyd's visit, it came to me that finally I heard things that I have been waiting for a long time. I embraced the feeling of being called "Aunt Ann" from Fred's nephew. Not once did my children ever get comforted from any of the Fischer Family during the time they lost their father. It was just take, take, take, and try to take more.

When Fred just passed away, Bruce was like the little man of the family. He kept watch over me, and stayed close by my side, I had the feeling that Bruce was afraid of losing me too. I had taken Fred's death very hard. I lost forty-two pounds in the first two months after Fred passed. My parents were very worried about me. I wasn't eating or sleeping at nights. I couldn't think straight and not concerned for myself. I would walk down town. I just wondered down town, aimlessly with nowhere definite to go. I just walked from one street to the next. I left my children in the care of my parents, I left the house in the morning and came back at night; I didn't care if I lived or died.

Again I came home from down town. The four children were sitting on the couch in the living room. My mother asked me where I was all day long. I told her that I was walking down town. My mother said, "Look right now at your four children. If you don't smarten up, and you keep on going like this, it won't take long before you make your four children orphans. Who would look after them?" "You had better look out for yourself and your children". "At our age we won't be able to look after them", scolding me.

I broke down and cried. That was a wake up call for me. I knew she was right. I looked at my four children sitting on the couch, I knew I needed to smarten up and stand up on my own two feet.

I played the evening of Fred's death over and over in my mind for years. The night that Fred said he would drop in at the Corona Hotel for a quick drink. The Corona was just a short distance from where my parent's house was. That night Fred's life had ended. Years later it was revealed to me what happened that night in the Corona. Fred walked into the door of the bar, two bachelors from the Golden Prairie area spotted Fred. They called Fred over to their table. The two bachelors ordered each another beer, they had been in the bar drinking already for some time. When Fred sat down at the table, he was handed a beer. After a few sips from his drink, Fred headed toward the washroom. The two poured hard liquor into Fred's beer… just for fun. It was known that the two had a mickey of rye tucked in their jackets. They had their fun, and Fred was carried away in a hearse that night. Fred couldn't handle hard liquor with all his allergies he had. He also didn't have any supper that night, and was drinking on an empty stomach. That cost him his life that night. I cannot put the blame on those two men that evening. Fred was not a child, and he should have known better. The next day the two men heard of the tragic news of Fred's death, and leaving a widow and four children behind.

I thought maybe they would be feeling sorry for their part, responsible for their actions that helped to take a father and husbands life. My daughter Melinda blamed herself for her fathers' death for years. She had said, "If I only would have not said I wanted to visit grandpa and grandma that night… maybe just maybe dad would still be here. We would have gone straight home." What a horrible burden for a child to carry for all those years!

Looking Back

It was coincidental that one of the men's fathers had passed away the same night that Fred died. I wonder if he felt bad drinking the same night his father died. Both funerals were held on the same day.

This is written the way it was told to me. It still bothers me how things unfolded that evening. I often wonder how our lives would have turned out had Fred still been here. My children wonder if their lives would have turned out differently than they are now. I honestly think if Fred could look back now, he would feel such shame. He would be heartbroken to see what his family had to endure. Fred would have been so proud watching his children grow up. He missed so much. He missed seeing his children through good times and bad, and missed out on his future grandchildren.

A Time For Healing

After the estate was settled, I had received my share of the estate. The children's share went to the Official Guardian of Saskatchewan until they each turned eighteen years of age.

My brother Adolf had his own construction business - A. Roth Construction. He helped me to make sure that I would be able to have my own home.

It was hard for my parents having four small children and myself living with them. They were elderly and were not accustomed to all the hustle and bustle of children. It was equally hard for my children; they were not allowed to have the freedom that they were so used to on the farm.

The city had just opened lots in a new development, and Adolf purchased a lot for me. Adolf started construction and by spring of 1971, we moved into our first home in Medicine Hat. The house cost me the better part of my share of the estate. I didn't care. We had a roof over our heads; it was warm in the winter. We walked on the plywood floor until I was able to afford floor coverings. My parents were happy that we were finally on our own.

I think Fred would have been proud of the achievements that my children and I made. The children worked hard helping

Looking Back

with house chores and yard work. They didn't even have to be told, they just saw the work, and did it. And better yet, the farm still stands there today. I have to admit that for as long as I was working, my two girls, Melinda and Audrey were the biggest helpers. After we had moved to Medicine Hat, I was lucky to have worked with a woman at a drapery shop. Ruby and I went into business on our own, and later I bought her share, and went out on my own, as Fischer's Draperies. Audrey worked with me at the shop after she graduated from high school. She was a fabulous sewer. Melinda was good with numbers, and she got a job at the Bank of Nova Scotia.

After ten years of absolutely no communication with the Fischer's, I was surprised by an invitation from my husband's sister Clara Gomke to attend Christmas supper on their farm in Hilda, AB. I discussed the invite with the children, hesitantly; we all agreed that it would be better to attend. After all I guess this was the first step to reconciliation.

It felt strange to be there, we had not much to talk about. We hadn't seen Clara and Edwin for so long. I noticed that Clara did most of her talking to the children; I guess it was easier to face them than it was to face me.

I was glad that Carl and Alice Fischer with their family were also invited. This eased the tension a bit. After supper Carl and Alice decided to return to Medicine Hat, and we followed suit; as I wanted to follow Carl's vehicle just in case there was car trouble. I had since learned how to drive the car Fred so cherished. It was the middle of winter, and I was glad that we arrived safely at home.

A few months passed and I decided to return the gesture and invited Clara, Edwin, Carl and Alice and their families for supper. Everything went smoothly. After supper I noticed my son Dale didn't appear for supper at all. Clara had gone down to the basement after she learned that Dale never ate. Clara started talking to Dale, but she was cut off short. "Why did you take the organ away from the girls", Dale was asking in a forceful tone in his voice. Clara stood there in shock; she didn't expect what came out of a timid little boy's mouth. She couldn't say a word; she turned away and returned upstairs, not mentioning a word of what went on minutes earlier. I wasn't aware until later what had happened. Dale told me himself what he had said to Clara.

"Mom" Dale spoke silently. "I was so hurt and angry that night", he continued. He still remembered the night we visited Clara at the farm. He observed Clara closely that evening. Clara hadn't spoke to you mom all night long. "I felt so sorry for you mom", Dale said. "I could see on your face you were covering up your hurt, I was thinking, what are we doing here?"

Dale never showed up for the whole evening. That same evening unexpectedly Edwin asked me about our land. He asked if I was willing to rent the land to him. I then realized why they were being friendly. Not to rekindle the relationship, but after the land once again. I didn't know that my current renter was giving up the land lease. Edwin had known before I had that my current renter was giving it up. So Edwin was inquiring about renting the land.

I didn't know at the exact moment what to do. Edwin made me an offer to rent the land, so I thought it would be alright. I knew Edwin was a hard worker and a good farmer. I thought I could trust Edwin as a renter.

There was a farmer in the Seven Persons area. His last name was Basil. He had a few quarters of land for sale. My brother-in-law, Carl Fischer who farmed in the same area was interested in buying the land. Carl had two sons who would be farming when they grew up. But Carl felt that the asking price of ninety thousand dollars a quarter was a bit too high in the 1980's. Edwin's son farmed in the Seven Persons area also wanted the same two quarters. Edwin's son was afraid that Carl would be the first to purchase the land, quickly gave Basil the asking price of $90,000 per quarter. Edwin did most of the work alone on our land. Harvey seemed to help out during the busiest times of the season, which was seeding and harvesting. The rest of the time he worked in a machine shop in Medicine Hat.

I often wondered why the Fischer family had never found time to see how I was doing with my four children. Now after ten years they had now suddenly taken interest, but their motives were after the land.

During harvest the quota had opened to sell wheat to the elevator. During that time, we were entitled to half share of the wheat sold. Harvey told me that if I wanted my cheque, it would be lying on the seat of his truck if it gets stolen it would not be his responsibility. I would send Audrey to pick up the cheque right away. I thought then and there that it was a huge mistake to have rented the land to them as I had then realized that the renter was not Edwin. I was relieved when the contract had ended. I had written them a letter telling them that the contract was over and they were to be off the land in the New Year.

My children asked me why I rented the land to them in the first place. They never knew where we were before. We didn't need them now.

I thought it would be in the best interest for my children to stay in good terms with their relatives, but now I saw it didn't matter. I could see the hatred and greed had never left the Fischer's. Fred's land was for my four children and I, and they never could get over that.

My children were affected deeply. Still today they ponder what would it have been like if things didn't transpire as it did. To myself the question was, "Why Me"? I understand it was hard to lose a brother, but it was more of a concern for them to have the Fischer homestead.

As up to this date, the Fischer Homestead still sits since the passing of Fred. For over forty years, the farm sits with fond memories overlooking the bountiful crops. It is the chosen place for summer picnics and time away from the busy city. To see my children and grandchildren happily enjoying the country farm air makes me happy. I'm sure their father and grandfather is watching over them. The memories will be there forever. Audrey and Melinda always saying…, "Hi Dad".

With hard work and long hours, I was fortunate to have been able to start my own drapery business. I was in business for over thirty years operating under the name of "Fischer's Draperies".

At that time we were doing a lot of work for the British Army in Ralston, AB. We had the contract with them for over twenty years making drapes in the family homes, offices and right in the Base itself. I loved working with the families. The people were easy going and we always did our best to have happy customers.

I was lucky to have a fantastic seamstress. Louise Bartmanovitz. She was a great help as she had many years of experience in the drape manufacturing business. In time my sister Hilda moved to Medicine Hat from Prince George, BC. She was always creative and her talents showed in the many different designs of cushions she made. Her other duties was to do the pressing, steaming and training of drapes.

I could have not been as successful as I was without Audrey and Melinda's help. Without them it would have been impossible to carry on for as long as I did.

Re-United

As time passed we received messages from our loved ones from Siberia through the Red Cross. They were able to come out of Siberia after over thirty years after WW11 had ended. I didn't waste time. My father had by this time passed away, and I knew deep in my heart that my dad would have said to me, "Anna, you go and visit". Go see them in Germany and be reunited with the ones who had survived. My father would have been so proud of me to go and visit our relatives. Had he been alive, I'm sure I would have had to tell him every detail, word for word.

It was 1982; Melinda and I purchased our plane tickets to Germany to be reunited to my relatives. My first visit was going to be my cousin Amalie Korb (nee Schortzman).

It was in 1944 that we had parted from our home place from the Ukraine. I had immigrated to Canada in 1951 from Germany, and the first to visit back to Germany in 1982. It was exactly thirty-eight years; I was excited to see Amalie and her family. Also one more cousin from my mother's side had arrived in Germany and was living in the southern part in Phullendorf, Germany.

One more reason to going to Germany was my son Dale was awarded a three-month scholarship from SAIT University. He had the best mark in the German language. For two months he went to work with different nationalities in a youth camp, and for one month he would be able to tour Germany. When I spoke to Dale over the telephone, I felt that he was very homesick, and I was planning to pay him a visit while in Germany. I was also anxious to meet cousins who were living in the southern part of Germany. I had known him by the name of Jacob Demjanenko, but he was now under the name of Jacob Himmelspach. I knew the name change occurred in Russia while going in hiding. Russian names were chosen to hide their identities. My first thought was that Jacob took on a German surname because of living in Germany. Many mixed nationality marriages, often the German name was taken weather it was the woman's or man's name, it didn't matter. It was easier to get a job with a German name than a Russian name in Germany. I guess I would find out upon visiting Jacob and his family in Pfullendorf, close to the camp was my son was in the region of the Black Forest (Schwarzwald). I was hoping that Jacob could take up to see Dale in the student camp.

When we notified them that we will be arriving in Germany, naturally everyone was excited, and waiting for our arrival. Dale was especially excited, being away from home for so long in a foreign country and homesick on top of it all.

The arrangements were all made, and Melinda and I boarded the Lufthansa to Germany. I couldn't wait to meet all my cousins that I hadn't seen for thirty-eight years. At the airport in Frankfurt, my cousins were waiting for us.

After Melinda and I made it through security, we picked up our luggage from the conveyer belt. I looked up and there was my cousin Amalie, her daughter Lenchen and her son-in-law Bodo. They decided to come and greet us at the airport. I cannot put into words how happy we all were to see each other. We were crying for joy. Amalie said to me, "Anna, thank God we are alive so we are able to see each other". Bodo blurted out,

Looking Back

"Tante Anna, we are taking you and Melinda sight seeing along the Rhine Valley".

It was just the beginning summer months in Germany. We drove, and by evening we arrived at Amalie's home in the area called Sauerland. Amalie's husband had also passed away, so Amalie and I had lots in common being both widows. As our journey ended for the day, we all were exhausted from the long trip and the excitement. But this didn't stop Amalie and I to stop our endless talking. Amalie told me that Bodo and Lenchen were going to take Melinda tomorrow morning with their motor home (wohnen vagen) and travel Germany, and her and I would visit Amalie's brother Albert and her mother Ottilie. This would be my Aunt Ottilie. I knew all these people from back home in our village of Johannestal, Ukraine. I soaked all the information in like a sponge. I wanted to know everything that happened in their past. I wanted to find out if there were more survivors from the terrible time we had to endure in our old home under the brutality through Communism and Stalin's criminal actions that was inflicted to millions of our innocent people.

Aunt Ottilie was sitting holding my hands tight in hers. This is the conversation we had:

> "Anna you sill remember after Emmanuel died"? Emanuel was her first husband and Amalie and Albert's real father, Emmanuel Schorzman. "Anna, how many evenings you had spent in the Schorzman house. Anna that was where your mother was raised from a small child on", Aunt Ottilie told me. "Your mother wasn't treated fairly by Grandma Schorzman", she recalled. Grandpa Schorzman was a good-hearted man. He did not like the way Grandma treated your mother.
>
> Grandma Schorzman was always complaining, your mom never could do anything right. Grandpa Schorzman replied back, "Why do you

always complain, can't you see that girl works all day long from morning to night. Your mother told Grandma Schorzman, "If I don't do something right for you, please spank me if that makes you feel better". Grandma became angrier. Your mother worked and most times Magdalena, their oldest daughter beautified herself, waiting for her boyfriend to arrive. Your mother from eight years of age was already making bread, and milking cows. Many times your mother was sitting milking the cow, and her thin arms too weak to finish. Emanuel, their youngest son, helped your mother when she wasn't able to finish.

Grandma Schorzman did not favor me because I was a poor girl. I had no assets to bring into the Schorzman estate".

Aunt Ottilie smiled, and continued with her story.

"After Emmanuel was allowed, we got married. I brought in to the Schorzman estate one beautiful little girl, Amalia, also a little granddaughter for them".

Amalie and I were best friends in our home living in our village of Johannestal. I still remember the death of Amalie and Albert's father Emmanuel. Aunt Ottilie remarried Karl Kurz and they together had two more children, Anna and Johan Kurz. Ottilie said that Karl was drafted into the German Army run by Hitler. He was fortunate to fall into the western allies as a prisoner of war. Aunt Ottilie was deported along with her four children to Siberia. She was so thankful for her two eldest children Amalie and Albert, as they helped raise the two younger siblings. Without them they may have all perished. Aunt Ottilie had the chance to be reunited with her husband in Germany.

Looking Back

Aunt Ottilie was heart-broken that Amalie and Albert were treated unfairly by the Kurz family. They lost their father's inheritance they would have received. They just wanted to keep peace within the family. Johan came away the best with the money from Ottilie's share from the Kurz and Schorzman. With the money they had built a beautiful two-story brick home. Ottilie's wish was that both Albert and Johan would live in the same home with their families. This didn't happen, and she was forced to be quiet and keep the peace.

It was now time for me to go and I could see tears streaming down Aunt Ottilie's cheeks. Amalie and I left and drove back to Amalie's house. We had the house to ourselves. Melinda, Lenchen and Bodo were to arrive in a couple of days. Amalie and I were planning to visit her brother and his wife Helene after breakfast in the morning.

Albert and Helene were happy to see us. Many years had gone by since we last seen each other. It was a wonderful reunion. After we got through the emotional greeting, we had lots to talk about.

After the war ended on May 8, 1945, the German refugees were called the "Volks-Deutsche" (Germans that were not born in Germany). The German people born in Germany were called the "Reichs-Deutsche".

Amalie was telling of the experience with the Russians. She began:

> "By the Russians, we were driven from all directions. Driven like cattle into the crammed barracks in Poland. By night we were all laying on the barrack floor, packed in like sardines in a tin can. Almost every night the Polish and Russian soldiers would come and shone their flashlights on the people sleeping on the floor. They would shine the flashlights in the faces looking for the young girls. They would drag the girls with them

screaming and kicking out of the barracks. The soldiers sexually molested and raped these girls. I was thankful that my mother gave me some good advice. We smeared our faces with sod, tied a kerchief around our heads and each held one of the younger children tightly against our bodies. I was told that I needed to look like a mother with a child. I was only 17 years old at the time. I could have been one of the unlucky girls. The Russian solders avoided the cries of the small children.

We were not able to stop the cry for help from the young girls as they were being pulled away from their parents and families. There was no help and nowhere to go for help. The screams and cries echoed through the night. Then the polish started their revenge, taking it out on innocent people. We could see the hatred against the Germans. Hitler in 1939 made an agreement with Stalin to remove the German people from Bessarabia and settle them in Poland. Many times the Polish people were chased off their land and the Bessarabian German people were placed on the land. The Polish had to work for the Bessarabian people, which was their own homestead before. This created much hatred.

As more and more people were packed into the barracks, there were promises to take us home where we originally came from. Back home, to the Ukraine. Instead the Polish took revenge and took their rage out on us innocent people. The Polish came to the barracks with horses and wagons. We were told they would take us to the train station to be deported to were we originally came from, our birthplaces. The people were trustworthy and vulnerable. Children, the elderly all were loaded on the wagons with their little belongings until the wagon was packed, ready to leave the barracks behind. In a short while they became aware that something was not right. The Polish took the wagons loaded with people deep into the forest. Once in the forest, all were chased off the wagons, their belongings taken from them. The wagons turned around and went the other direction. The people with the small children were left in the dark in the forest. They started to walk back toward the barracks. It had taken all night long for them to make their way back. Exhausted and crying children in tow, they arrived. Some of the elderly collapsed on the ground from exhaustion.

In a short time, the camps were overflowed with people. Then the clearing of the barracks came again. Again we were driven in heard to the freight train station in Poland. This time 40-50 or more people were loaded into boxcars. The floor of the boxcar was layered with a skiff of straw. There was no room to make a bed for the small children.

My mom was sitting on a small pail holding the two youngest on her lap. Albert and I were standing on each side of our mother to protect her from being pushed over by others. My mother started to cry saying, "I have a feeling we're not going home". The train pushed on forward. By morning people were complaining as it started to get colder inside the boxcar. We started to wrap ourselves in blankets or with whatever was available. I noticed frost had started to build up in the metal boxcar. Our journey went on in its second day. The train slowly came to a stop. The door to the boxcar was opened from the outside. The door had been secured with wire so nobody was able to jump off. We were so happy that the door was open and in the boxcar, a couple of loaves of bread were thrown in to divide amongst all of us. I had the chance to look outside when the door was open. All I could see was heaven and snow.

Small packs of wolves were following the train tracks. At first I thought they were stray dogs. Someone said that they were wolves. Then we knew we were in the wilderness. We never knew where we were. The train didn't stop at the regular train stations, only at isolated locations.

The boxcars were filled with people from different villages from the Ukraine. The people from the same villages tried to be together in the same boxcars, but it didn't always work out. It just so happened that we had a family close to our home place by the surname of Ebel.

The woman's name was Erna with her four small children and her mother-in-law. They originated from the village of "Worms". Erna's husband was drafted into the German Army, and he was missing.

As the train again came to a stop, the doors opened from the outside. People could pee outside beside the train track. Then the call came for the dead ones to be brought out. I noticed that some dead people were taken off the train and were laid out on the ground. I made a remark to my mother as to how sad it was to see them being laid out in the open. My mother just nodded her head in agreement.

The second night Erna gave birth to her 5th child in the boxcar. We heard a loud squealing and then silence. The newborn had died the same night from the bitter cold. By now we were deep into the wilderness. The boxcar was wired shut from the outside, and we were powerless inside. Everyone was sitting close to each other, trying to keep warm off of each other. Many worries crossed each and every one's minds. Wondering what was to become of their lives.

We didn't cause the war, we didn't ask to be here, and why are we being so badly punished. The question of why was asked many times with no answer.

Again the boxcar opened and I looked out to see something, but nothing different, but sky, snow and the wilderness. All the people were allowed to get out of the boxcar to relieve themselves. A few loaves of bread were divided amongst ourselves. And again the call came for the dead. With time passing, more dead people were brought out of the boxcar. On signal everyone had to board the boxcar to continue eastward.

By now we were aware that Erna was hiding her dead infant's body covered up in the corner. She was hoping to bury her baby when the destination was reached.

Every time the doors opened, it was always the same. Snow, wilderness, and the dead, thrown out. Packs of wolves still followed behind the train tracks. The wolves were following us for a reason. They knew food for them was being left behind in the snow. They could smell the scent of death for miles. Some of us children were well aware of having more than the newborn's dead body in the boxcar. The elders were whispering and hiding something, not to let anything to slip out. They were afraid that the children would slip out the secret they were trying so desperately trying to hide.

Days went by and the doors opened again and again. The call for the dead ones to be brought out. By now the people in the boxcar were panicking. I could see the sorrow in my mother's eyes. Erna and her mother-in-law cried. Their cries started the entire boxcar of other women crying. Erna with her mother-in-law started laying out four of her five children out on the snow. The newborn and three of the youngest children; the oldest survived. Erna fell on her knees in front of her dead children, crying uncontrollably. People stood along the train for as far down as you could see. The dead lying on the snow. Cries of the people, who had lost their loves ones. Others cried for each other's pain. It was so inhumane as to how the bodies were laid out in the open for the wolves to treat themselves. Erna had to be dragged away from her children and taken into the boxcar.

In Russian the soldiers hollered, "Don't cry, somebody will come and take the bodies for burial". Nobody spoke. No one had to. It was known that the wolves were following for a reason. The people in the boxcars did not believe what the Russians were telling them to believe. No way would somebody come from civilization into the wilderness, in no mans land to pick up the bodies of children and the elderly".

I listened intently on every word that Amalie spoke. Images went through my mind of the suffering these people had to go through. My heart went out to the families; one can only imagine the torment they went through.

Amalie continued.

"After almost living in the boxcar for one week, the train came to a stop. The train engine had quit working. In a short time the train maneuvered back and forth. You could hear the clanging of the trains connecting to the engine car. Finally the door opened, cans were used to pee in. Outside the same thing was seen, the sky up above, and the snow on the ground, and the wilderness surrounding us.

We knew deep down that our destination was Siberia. It was hoped that there we would find food, a warm place to lay our heads, and peace.

Finally our destination had been reached. We were all relieved to get out of the boxcars. It was terribly cold in the Siberian winter. We were then loaded onto trucks, which took us to the barracks. The barracks were cold. For as far as your eyes could see were massive rows of barracks.

Anna Fischer

We soon realized we were sent there to work... slavery. The regime was trying to suck us dry. We were now prisoners to the Russians. It was estimated that more than one thousand people perished during the long train trek to Siberia. The wild wolves were well nourished; they fed on the dead bodies laid on the snow, left behind.

We were crammed in the barracks like cattle going to slaughter. In the middle of the barrack stood a metal barrel with a pipe, which lead out to the roof. This was to burn branches that were picked. This would provide some heat. We weren't allowed to cut any trees for heating the barracks, only branches that lay on the ground. Some were living in old oil tanks.

We were informed of the work that was to be done in the forest. We were divided into groups. Early morning the call sounded along the barracks. "*Davy Davy, roboda*" (come on out to work). We had no identity there; we were just numbered like animals.

We worked in the forest all day cutting trees. By evening we looked forward to find a warm place in the barracks. The children were left alone in the barracks all day while the adults worked. The children had to learn fast how to survive on their own during the day.

The younger people were called in for interrogations, so many questions were asked. They wanted to know what went on in our homes and villages while being occupied by the German Nazis. Who belonged to the BDM (*Bund Deutsche*

Looking Back

Madchen – Pure German Girls)? Who were involved in the Hitler youth? What were the German teachers' names? He wanted to know the names of the young men that belonged to the Notwehr (self-defense). The names of people that had freely joined the Germans to help fight against the Soviet regime.

I didn't have answers to their questions. I persisted with answering, "I don't know". I knew what it meant if I mentioned any names. We were young and such matters didn't interest me. My interrogation went for hours. The longest interrogation took eight hours. Back in the barrack, my mother became very worried, she feared that I would be locked up or taken away.

By the time I was able to go back to the barrack, daylight was nearing. My mother walked the barrack floor all night until my return. My mother imagined the worse. Both my mother and I were deprived of our sleep. As I returned to the barrack, the call came for us to go to work in the forest. We worked from early morning until evening. We left in the dark and came back to the barrack in the dark. The walk was sometimes up to 3 km into the forest to cut trees. By evening we were exhausted and cold and wet. Many times we didn't even undress. Our stockings were drying on our bodies during the night. We had no other clothing to change into. We had just the clothes on our back. After a short time of living in the barracks, we all were infested with lice".

"Anna", Amalie said to me. "It is true; I could swear that when I came back to the barracks from my day's work, when I took off my stockings, they would move from all the lice.

Amalie picked up the conversation where she left off.

"To get the lice under control, the only solution was to pour boiling water over our clothes. The knitted wool socks couldn't be deloused or they would shrink. Then they would be useless. Any spare moment was spent sitting and lousing each other's hair.

On the other side of their barracks were barracks filled with prisoners of war, mostly from Germany. They too in the early morning hours had to form a long line ready to go to work. It was sad to see how they stood shivering from the cold. They were hungry and their faces looked as if they had never slept through the night. It took hours to warm up from being outside all day, and finally would fall asleep to do the same all over the next day.

The German prisoners had no warm clothing for the Siberian winter. Some wrapped themselves in blankets. Hunched over, you could see ice cycles begin forming under their noses. It was so pitiful to see how humans could treat each other. Every time I looked their way, I couldn't help but cry.

Everyday more and more people were arriving to the barracks. More accommodations were being needed. Now spring of 1947 arrived, and we noticed the prisoners were taken out of their barracks to make room for the new families coming.

Looking Back

The German soldiers were digging holes in the ground. Placing several layers of tree branches over the holes then would put dirt on top. In these holes is where the prisoners lived. It was just awful to see the prisoners living in the ground like gophers. Each morning you could see them emerging from the ground. The Russian regime didn't see the prisoners as human beings; they were treated like animals. Their living conditions were horrendous".

It took over ten years until the German Counselor; Dr. Adenauer had his first visit to Russia. The German counselor had brought up the fate for the German prisoners and the German people to give them more freedom. The freedom rights had still dragged on for years until it was all done.

Stalin considered himself as "Josep Vissironavich Dzhugachvili" (Made of steel). He died in March of 1953 of a massive brain hemorrhage. He was 73 years old. This gave hope for millions of Germans including Ukrainians and Russians.

Two years after Stalin's death, and ten years after WW11 ended, it was announced that German Counselor Dr. Adenauer had talked to Russia's leader Nikita Krushev about the inhumane living conditions in the camps. The Germans were removed from captivity and given the chance to return to their birthplace and home place in Germany. But the German people born in the Ukraine or Russia were not so lucky. The process went slowly. It took more discussions between Adenauer and Krushev to release these people and give them their freedom to return to their homes in Germany. In the region where they were working, if their quota was filled, only then were they allowed to try to receive permission to leave Russia. Amalie told me that it took many walks to the Russian authorities, begging for permission to go to Germany. From millions of our German people, there were only a small percentage of survivors that had been deported. There was much desperation to try to get out of Russia. Most of them found their fate in the Russian wilderness.

During my time visiting with Amalie, I was surprised to hear that Waldemar Zimmerman along with his family were also lucky to escape Siberia and return to Germany. Waldemar's mother, Christina was a relative to my father, she was born a "Roth".

I was anxious to meet as many people as possible during my stay. After all we haven't seen each other since our departure out from our home and birth land, the Ukraine since 1944. Thirty-eight years have gone by since I last saw Waldemar and we were so happy to see each other again. At the moment it was all like a dream. I never had given up hope and prayed at least to see and meet some of our people again. I had hoped deep in my heart that God would answer my prayers. I was not forgotten; God had answered my prayers, a dream that came true.

Amalie, Melinda and I were listening to Waldemar's experience during the war. Waldemar was nick named Wowa (Vova) back home in the day. Wowa (Vova) was only fifteen years old at the time when he left Johannestal behind. Waldemar was revealing the same happenings as I had heard from others.

Waldemar began his story:

> "When we were deported from the barracks in Poland, we were driven like herds of cattle to the freight train station. We were packed like sardines in a can. The promises we were given were to be taken home to our village of Johannestal, Ukraine. But it wound up to be heading deep in the northeasterly direction.
>
> It got colder and colder by the hour. Bodies were being taken out of the long haul boxcars. The train was moving slowly, was it to dump more dead bodies before we reached our destination? Nobody knew.

Looking Back

I along with other boys were taken and rerouted to a different destination, my route was heading toward the Ural Mountains. When we finally stopped in the wilderness we ended up in Karaganda were there were rows and rows of barracks. The barracks were so cold and very little to eat. One good thing, we were working in the coalmines. I was one of the youngest German prisoners of war. Several months after working in the coal mine, there was a huge explosion. It took many lives. The rescue operation immediately brought out people. This process took several days; the ones injured or still living were taken to the hospital. The ones that showed no life or were dead were taken and laid out on the floor in a large building. I was amongst the dead list. I lay on the floor for three days; I was going in and out of consciousness. The days came for burial of the dead, and were to be loaded. When it came to me, they realized that I showed signs of life. I was hurt badly and taken to the hospital and under a doctor's care.

From that coalmine explosion, my whole body including my face and head and eyes was imbedded with coal fragments under the skin. The doctors started to begin to remove the coal splinters and do skin grafting. The coal imbedded into my skin couldn't be removed. They had become part of my skin. If I had been brought to the hospital right away, the chances of recovery would have been better. Now I was totally blind after spending several months in the hospital.

I was released from the hospital, and I relied on my seeing-eye dog. I attended many visits to the eye specialist. The doctors and specialists had to report on my progress, if any. I was received monthly pay as I was no longer able to work".

Oh how the communist government would have loved to take that money away from me. I had to attend each and every appointment so the government would know of my condition.

Being blind is a terrible life to live."

Waldemar with tears in his eyes said to me, "Anna, I was many times suicidal and made many attempts to end my life. I cannot quite grasp how I survived. Something inside of me told me... no Waldemar you're too young to die".

Waldemar continued with his story.

"One day, in a split second, I saw a spark of daylight, and then it was gone. I was so excited that I shared the good news with the doctor on my next appointment. The doctor filed the report on my progress to the regime. Then my sick pay was cut. That was my reward for being honest. If I knew what I didn't know, I would have kept my mouth shut. I always wanted to believe that honesty takes you through life. I think there is something behind all of this. I had the chance to get out of my darkest part of my life, and come home to Germany. I'm living a peaceful life with my family. I am sad that I lost my mother, father and brother to starvation in Siberia".

Waldemar with a smirk on his face said to me, "You see Anna, I live like this now. A friend asked me what I was doing today and I replied, "Nothing". My friend said that I did the same thing yesterday".

Looking Back

"Oh", I said, "I didn't finish yet".

Waldemar sat chuckling with a big smile on his face. .

Waldemar had lived a peaceful life in Germany until the time of his passing, where he joined his parents and his brother Gottlieb.

It was now time to go south and visit my son Dale in Germany. He was there through his scholarship, and was working at the youth camp in the Black Forest. My cousin Jakob Himmelspach was living in Phullendorf, West Germany not too far from where Dale was. Melinda and I took the bus and went south to visit Jakob and his family first. They had been deported to Siberia and were just living in Germany for only a few short years. Jakob told of his experience in Siberia. His mother was severely burned when a gasoline jug she was carrying exploded, leaving her scarred for life. The next day I asked Jakob if he would take us to where Dale was in the camp.

Dale was so happy to see us. I could see that he was so very homesick. We spent several hours with Dale. There was so much to talk about. Dale was explaining to us what he had to do while in the camp. He couldn't wait until his two months were up. Dale said one day he was talking to a very nice lady, and the next day she came and brought with her little girl and a bottle of wine and some cookies. Dale thought that the lady sensed that he was homesick and wanted to cheer him up.

I could see tears in Dale's eyes when it was time to part. It seemed that he couldn't let us go and be left behind. So it was not easy to part. We had spent the afternoon with Dale, and Jakob was eager to return home.

Jakob worked in a *holzschnitzerei* (wood carving factory). As we entered the car, Dale came and gave us one more hug saying, "Mom, I wish I could go home with you". I broke down and cried.

Dale walked away crying as well. We had approximately one and a half hours to drive back, and we all were tired and needed rest.

Anna Fischer

The next morning I asked Jacob why he had changed his name from Demjanenko to Himmelspach. Jacob said to me:

"Anna, it's a long story and I wouldn't blame you if you don't believe what I'm going to tell you. When we were being deported from Poland to Siberia, we were crammed into the cold barracks. People were looking to find their loved ones. Jakob was separated from his mother and siblings and taken by the Germans to dig shelters. I had been loaded on a different train with other deportees. Jakob was asking other people where they were from. He was not familiar with anybody. Finally an elderly lady asked me who I was and where I was from. I told her that I was Jakob Demjanenko from Johannestal. The lady was so happy to hear where he came from. She blurted out that she was Mrs. Eberhardt and was from Landau. The two villages were not very far apart. The lady told me that she knew many people in Johannestal. Year's back she used to live in Johannestal before moving to Landau. She asked me if by chance, was your mom Kraus Philip's daughter by the name of Hanna Krause"?

Jacob said to me, "Anna, I was in shock, and I couldn't say a word".

"Mrs. Eberhardt also mentioned that the Krause's had 1 daughter that was not so swift. She was kind of slow. Her name was Dina. Mrs. Eberhardt said that she told me that she knew many people from Johannestal. Your father was also named Jacob, but he was called Jasha. Little Jasha, your father was approximately 5 – 6 years old when your grandma Maria gave him to people who had no children, Peter and Katharina Schatz.

192

Looking Back

Now I couldn't help but cry. Word for word that this woman was telling me was the truth. I gave this old woman a hug. She was lonesome and alone too. I called her my aunt in the Russian language. I could not leave her side. I wanted to know more. Mrs. Eberhardt was saying there was more for me to know about my father. I was eighteen years of age, all alone and she wanted to share her knowledge about my family. She was in her 80's and also parted from her family. Mrs. Eberhardt told me that if she didn't tell me, I would never find out.

Mrs. Eberhardt told me that she needed to tell me something else. She said that your father's name was not Demjanenko. I shouted, "Who am I"? The old lady told me that she knew my grandmother Maria personally. Maria was working for rich landowners by the name of Jakob Himmelspach in Landau. Mrs. Eberhardt didn't know Maria's last name. All she knew was that after her parents had starved, Maria was left alone. After her parents starved to death, she walked from village to village looking for work. She found work at the Himmelspach Estate in Gute. She was never asked her last name, it didn't matter. Maria was called "little Maria". Maria was loved by everyone; she was an *fleissiges madchen* (hard working girl). Maria was a beautiful girl, but poor, she wore her inheritance on her face.

The young Jakob Himmelspach fell in love with Maria. Getting married for the both of them was slim as Maria was very poor. Your grandma Maria was pregnant with your father. Before the child was born, Maria got to know a homeless man by the name of Demjanenko, so Jacob, your father took on the name of Demjanenko for fear of losing her child. This was kept a big secret. Maria was still working with the Himmelspach family. Five years later, Demjanenko died of the influenza that was widespread in the area. Maria was not able to work and keep a child in those days. Maria gave the little boy to the Schatz family. Little Jakob became their little cow herder. To keep your job was very important for survival, and Jakob was called "little Jasha" and that's the way it stayed.

Times were changing and the civil war was creeping up in many parts of the country. It was said by the people, "the reds are fighting the white, and the white are fighting the red".

At the time it seemed the country rapidly got more and more unstable. The rich landlords started to go in hiding. And your grandma Maria was now a young widow.

Maria was still working for the Himmelspach family. Young Jakob Himmelspach and Maria kept their promise to each other that they would be married some day. Then again she became pregnant with Jacob's second child. Again the pregnancy was kept a secret. Maria was terrified of losing her child as there were rumors leaking out of the pregnancy. In her fright, Maria packed her little bit of belongings in the middle of the night and walked ten km to Johannestal. March 1904, Maria had landed on the doorstep of a man that she knew by the name of Myron Belanov. Myron was working for rich landowners in Johannestal. Maria found work for the rich people cleaning their homes.

Maria gave birth to a baby girl. Maria was so frightened of losing her girl right after the baby was born. Myron and Maria went to register the baby's birth. So the baby girl adopted the surname of Belanov. Mrs. Eberhardt said that Myron was a very nice good-hearted man, and accepted the little baby as his own. The little girl was named Ottilie (Otaria).

I asked Mrs. Eberhardt to clarify that Otaria was my father's sister. Both had different names and conceived from the same man Himmelspach. I told Mrs. Eberhardt that my father and Tante Otaria knew they were siblings, they knew of their mother Maria, but never found the connection of their father, Jakob Himmelspach. In a few years later the whole Himmelspach family had disappeared, nobody knew what had happened to them. Where they deported? Did they go in hiding? Maybe they had the chance to go abroad. They were branded as the "Kulak". Maria would never have given her children their real name of Himmelspach for fear of being deported. It was dangerous to be classified as a Kulak. If Maria would have been deported along with the two children had not taken the Himmelspach name for her children. All would have been tagged as Kulak.

Now you know who you are she told me. Your grandma and I knew each other well. I visited with Maria and Myron often. They were a happy couple with their little girl. After three years of marriage Myron passed away from influenza. Typhus was a bad killer in those days. Maria dragged her little girl along everywhere she worked. Maria at the time went with the thrashing crew harvesting. The thrashing machine moved from one place to the next. The Schortzman Family set up the thrashing machine. Maria was very good at setting the sheaves. As the straw was pulled up a horse on either side, when Maria was caught by the iron cable, and was dragged and fell approximately thirty meters from the highest peak to her death. The Schorzman family felt so sorry for the little girl, Otaria. They had taken her in, not to cuddle and nurture her, but for a work slave. The Schorzman family arranged Maria's funeral. The Schorzman family never sent Otaria to school. Both my mother and her brother Jakob were illiterate".

I still remember as a young child, when the communist regime had taken away all our property and livestock. Our crop and vineyards now all belonged to the government. The only ones belonging to the separate group called *"Krasna Hura"* (Red Flag). These people were doing dangerous work underground in the stone quarry. This group was able to keep their vineyards. So my Uncle Jacob's family was allowed to make wine and had their grapes to eat. I remember as a young girl, I was helping harvesting the grapes. I was in heaven for a day. We ate grapes, as many as we could. After the harvest of the grapes, they were delivered to the Schatz family where my Uncle Jakob was raised. They still had their wine press and barrels in their cellar. If Uncle Jakob received a few bottles of wine, then he was lucky.

Uncle Jakob was working for years in the Stone Quarry. In 1942 the mine caved in and the mineworkers were buried under

Looking Back

the rubble. Rescue crews came to rescue the miners. Uncle Jakob was rescued, and brought up from the mine and taken to the hospital in Landau in our neighboring village. Unfortunately he died, leaving his family behind.

From then on the Schatz's like before, helped them selves by harvesting Jacob's grapes and sold the wine for their own profit. My Uncle's family never received anything. My mother often told my Aunt Hanna not to let this go on, but Hanna didn't want to do anything against the Schatz's. Hanna stayed on with her four children and one sister that was handicapped and was not able to work. As long as Jakob was alive they were able to afford bread to eat, but now they were very poor. Sometimes Uncle Jakob brought my family a loaf of bread. Now that was over with.

In the early years poverty was everywhere in the world. People worked hard, and walked away with little to next to nothing at the end of the day. During those times, it was very hard to support a family.

My cousin Jacob said that he was in disbelief of the things he heard from Mrs. Eberhardt. But he knew it was true. Jacob said, "Every time I saw Mrs. Eberhardt in the barracks, I couldn't get enough information. I always struck up the same conversation".

Mrs. Eberhardt continued to tell me:

> "Jacob I told you what concerns you. I remember when you dad Jakob got married to Hanna Kraus. I was at the small gathering. The Krause family was large and very poor".

"In other words my father and his sister never had found out where they belonged to or who they were?" asked Jakob.

> "That's right, they never knew and they both died", replied Mrs. Eberhardt.

"You know Anna", Jakob said to me. "I never ever knew the old lady's first name. It wasn't important at the time I guess, nor did I once ask for Grandma Maria's family surname, the only thing I found out from Mrs. Eberhardt that our grandma Maria was born in 1874 and died in 1908 in Johannestal. She was known as the little Maria".

Now Jakob and I had talked and covered so much. It was late and Melinda was gone for the afternoon with Jakob's daughter. She also had the name Anna. The two of them went to meet with friends in the park.

Now this was our last stop with our people, and now we reached the end of our holiday. To me it was a very important reunion. So many years had lapsed. So many experiences were revealed. Wherever we went, the visits were emotional with many tears. It was sad to hear of the many loved ones who had perished through torture and hunger.

Now the time had come to part, and we headed to Frankfurt Air Port. We boarded the Lufthansa, and flew straight to Canada landing in the Calgary Airport. It was another three-hour drive back to Medicine Hat. We were glad to be home again with the rest of my family and they were happy to see us back again. I had left my other daughter Audrey in charge at the drapery business, and the work was piling up during the month that I was gone. We kept busy trying to catch up on the orders at work. Years had passed and I many times thought of the family members back in Germany.

I corresponded with family over the telephone. This communication was faster then by mail and a cheaper to keep in touch. And hopefully stay in touch. I remember a conversation with my cousin Jakob over the phone. I asked him to repeat the conversation again that he had with Mrs. Eberhardt. He began to retell everything, and I believe I had kept him on the phone for nearly two hours, while I was taking notes on the other end. By the end of our conversation, I told Jacob to be prepared for many more calls to come from me. It was when I had him repeat his story for the fourth time that he said to me, "Anna, how many more times do you want me to repeat the story about our parents? I told you over and over what I found out and know". Jacob confessed, "Anna, I don't blame you, I did the same thing to the poor lady Eberhardt".

Jakob told me that one day the Russians came to the barracks and took us younger boys away to work in the mines, and years later when the commander was taken away, it was then when Jakob started to search for his mother and the rest of his siblings. That was when the feeling of freedom was felt. Jakob was able to find his siblings and they were reunited, but his mother had died of starvation.

I still phone Jakob occasionally to see how he is doing. Jakob lost his wife Anna Marie, and now Jakob is living with his two daughters in the same home where they lived when we were visiting. I also stay in touch with my cousins Amalie Korb, Albert and his wife Helene and their mother Aunt Ottilie. I love them all very much, and they are just the few survivors' left from our home place. I feel we are all part of each other. I cannot describe the close feeling between us all. We all went through the same hardships, which brought us close together.

When speaking with Amalie, I was encouraging her to come to visit me in Canada. I was happy to hear that she decided to visit. I decided to surprise Amalie and purchased two tickets for us to fly to Las Vegas. She would have never had the chance to go there otherwise. The only thing was that it was in July, the hottest time of the year to be in Vegas.

Amalie arrived in Canada, and Melinda and I headed to Calgary airport to meet her. We waited for the huge plane to land. We saw the German Lufthansa coming to a landing. Waiting at customs, among all the passengers, we noticed Amalie. She came out to pick out her luggage; she looked so lost and scared. As soon as we got close to Amalie, she was so glad to see us. Amalie was worried sick at the thought of nobody being at the airport to meet her. She was so happy to be out of the airplane. Eight hours in the air, over the big ocean. Now it was time to part from the airport and head out for the three-hour drive to Medicine Hat. On the way Amalie noted, "My God, I feel like I came to Siberia". I asked her why she would say such a thing. "Because there are no villages, no people", she replied. We are driving on the No. 1 highway, which takes us from one end of Canada to the other. You see only some farms, abandoned buildings and Graineries along the highway. As we were passing through Strathmore, Amalie was so interested in everything she saw. I answered her inquisitive questions in detail. Amalie couldn't get over how much space we have in our homes compared to the little crammed suites she was used to in Germany. Everybody was tired and the time change for Amalie for sure was tiring for her.

My family knew of my visitor from Germany, and I was prepared for many visitors. All were just excited to meet this relative from Germany and many invites were made to go to their homes. My daughters kept the business going and I drove Amalie to introduce her to my cousins.

My big surprise day was nearing for Amalie. We got up one morning, and I told her we were going for a short trip. Melinda drove us back to Calgary airport again. Amalie was wondering where I was taking her. "Don't tell me, we are flying again", Amalie queried. She seemed frightened to be in the airplane. "I've arranged a little surprise for you", I beamed telling Amalie. "We both have gone through so much in our lives and this surprise is to show you the other side of the world. I think you'll like it, it will be something you have never seen before, and may never see again". I had the same experience years back and never regretted it, and I want you to experience the same. It made me feel like living in a dream, and I hope it makes you feel the same. We are staying for one week. Our accommodations were booked at the Hacienda Hotel.

We never went for the reason to gamble our hard earned money away. We enjoyed the scenery and the glitter of the night-lights. We even were able to take in a live show. I still remember seeing Tammy Wynette on stage. It was so beautiful. We were sitting in a perfect spot in the audience. We were even so lucky as to shake hands with the country and western singing star. It was the most wonderful night, a night to remember.

Amalie was so excited to see such a place. She had taken many pictures of Vegas to take back with her to Germany. I knew Amalie didn't have much money, and I was happy to do something special for Amalie.

Amalie and I were both widows, both in our mid 50's and in good health. Amalie was so fascinated with Las Vegas. She insisted that we walk the strip to see everything. I told her that it was impossible to walk in the July heat in Vegas. Again Amalie insisted that she wanted to walk. We had our breakfast in the hotel, and began our walk. Well it didn't take long before Amalie stopped and said, "Anna I'm burning up and I'm so thirsty". She needed water or anything wet to drink. We had no other choice but to go into the casino and pretend to play the machines to get our free drinks. We kept on our walk, but barely out of one casino and into the next for another cold drink. Finally it was so tiring that we took the shuttle bus back to our hotel. After supper Amalie was ready for bed, it was a long hot day. I exclaimed to Amalie, "the night life is just starting. In the night you see the most glitter of the lights". Amalie asked when does everyone get peace and quiet? I laughed and said, "Dear Amalie, this city never sleeps"!

Amalie was amazed at how beautiful was at night. We were sitting on the balcony just taking in the view. Wherever you looked you saw glittery lights flashing, and people.

Amalie said to me, "Anna, Las Vegas is for the rich, for the celebrities, models and dancers, there is so much to see. We don't belong here, we're just poor Germans". Amalie, you would be surprised to know haw many visitors come from Germany, and different countries around the world. They come from all over to see Vegas. Amalie just beamed, "Anna I thank you from the bottom of my heart for giving me such a wonderful holiday, this is the best holiday in my life and the only one I ever had".

Our one-week holiday came to an end and we took the bus to the Los Vegas airport. We boarded the plane and off we headed to Canada, landing in Calgary two hours later.

Melinda was at the airport waiting for us. On our way driving back to Medicine Hat, Amalie could not stop explaining to Melinda of all the exciting things she saw.

Amalie only had a short stay in Canada left, so we spent the rest of that time visiting so relatives could say their goodbyes. We took Amalie to the Calgary airport and saw her off to go back to Germany.

I received a phone call from Amalie's daughter. "*Tante Anna* (Aunt Anna), our mother arrived safely at the Frankfurt airport, we were waiting for her when the plane landed. Tante Anna, what have you done to our mother? Since she arrived back home, she can't keep her mouth shut. She talks of all the excitement that she had in Vegas. All we hear is Vegas, Vegas, and Vegas". With a slight chuckle in my voice I replied, "Lenchen I'm so glad that your mom had a nice holiday with all of us in Canada".

In the year 1996, I received news of one more loved one that came out of Siberia and was returned to Germany. I was so happy and excited so hear this news; it had been fifty-two years since we were parted. I wanted so much to go to where she lived, but I liked to have somebody to travel with me, but my two daughters were not able to take off work.

I thought that perhaps my brother Adolf and his wife Margaret would come with me to Germany. They said they would accompany me to Germany and we got our passports and documents ready. We boarded the flight from the Calgary airport by Lufthansa to Frankfurt.

On arrival to Frankfurt, I held up a sign reading the words, "*Frohes Wiedersehen nach 52 yahre* (Happy reunion after 52 years)" my cousin Rosa and her son Waldemar and her son-in-law noticed my sign. I honestly have to admit that I would never have recognized my cousin Rosa. So many years had passed between us. It was almost to say a lifetime. It was quite an emotional reunion at the airport. So many tears were shed. Thinking how happy our parents would be to see the opportunity granted to us to see each other after so many ears. It was sad to say a lifetime. With our visit with Rosa, I wanted to know so much about their life in Siberia, and her parents. Her mom was my father's sister. It was so sad; many of my questions were ignored. It seemed that Rosa didn't want to reveal her past. Rosa and her 14-year-old brother Rudolf had to dig their own parent's grave and bury their mother and father in the wilderness in Siberia. They died a horrible death due to starvation. So many of our people completely locked up their past internally. Being through the misery myself, I understand and could relate fully to the way they felt.

But deep in our hearts we know who we are to each other.

Rosa was living with her daughter Lisa and her family in the city of Wiesbaden, Germany. Lisa was a wonderful woman. For me I never regretted meeting Rosa's family, it was an honor and a lifetime opportunity to be in their presence.

During that same visit, another relative, Amalie Marchel (nee Roth) had come out of Siberia and arrived in Germany. It also was fifty-two years since we seen each other. I was determined to meet Amalie before we had to depart from Germany. Arrangements were made to have Amalie and Rosa reunited.

Amalie arrived and she was so happy to see us, and we were happy to see her. We held on to each other and tears of joy rolled down our faces. Amalie was telling us the familiar stored of the events of our German people. That after the war ended on May 1945, our German people were not able to escape from Poland to the west for safety to Germany. It was unbelievable how the Russians and the Polish were herding up the German people like cattle in the overfilled barracks. By nights the Russians came to the barracks disturbing the sleeping people and children, shining flashlights to their faces looking for the young girls, dragging them out of the barracks kicking and screaming. They were raped and molested, getting beaten until unconscious if they resisted.

My cousin Amalie Marchel said to me, "Anna, I'm not ashamed to tell you that it wasn't my fault". She started to cry.

"I was one of the many victims that had suffered through a night of rape. As the Russians were pulling me out of the barracks in the middle of the night, I was screaming as loud as I could. I screamed for help. My own mother was kneeling in front of them, begging for them to take her instead, and to spare her daughter from there no good intentions. But they beat my mother up that she was not able to walk. They dragged me by force. I screamed and resisted and I was beaten. I was taken to the barn and was raped by the Polish and Russians, and then they beat me unconscious. They left me lay in the barn underneath the straw.

In the early morning, women who came to milk the cows found me. As I was regaining consciousness, I didn't know where I was. All I knew was that I was in terrible pain and I couldn't see out of my eyes. My whole body was sore. My face was swollen and black and blue from the beating. The women from the barracks took me and washed my face, and laid me down to rest. After I could open my eyes and I looked in the mirror, I just cried. Did I deserve this?

Within the next few days, we were driven to the freight train station in Poland for deportation.

Looking Back

The promise we received was to be taken to our homes where we came from. In our boxcar we had mostly people from the Ukraine. But it ended up in false promises. The Russians took us to Siberia, to Novosibirsk Kasagsta Archangels and to the Ural Mountains. It was bitter cold; the sickly elderly and especially the small children weren't able to withstand the cold temperatures. It was estimated that more than one thousand people perished en route on our train to Siberia. Many more died of starvation in the barracks.

It was said that half of the German prisoners of was last their lives in the Russian Siberian Wilderness. Anna, you cannot even imagine the conditions we had to live in Siberia. Living in the barracks was inhumane. Even though many were starving, they still were forced out of the barrack to work in the forest. Some people lost their lives while at work. When someone died, they were buried in the deep snow. If the ground was thawed their fellow workers dug small graves. The distance to and from work was approximately three km one way".

I wanted so much for my cousins in Germany to come to Canada and visit. I begged them, and was willing to pay for their flight. I was hoping that they would agree to come and visit with the rest of their cousins in Canada. I wished that my parents could have had the joy of having this reunion after 52 years. My father passed away in 1979, and my mother passed away from cancer in 1984. My dad was so interested in knowing what became of relatives back in Germany and the ones in Siberia.

I can feel the pain that my parents had to endure in their lives to lose their brother and sister especially Heinrich, my father's youngest brother. The two of them were inseparable. They were very close especially in the time of living in the hardships and struggles of survival. Uncle Heinrich lost his wife Anna, leaving him with four small children to tend to.

It is sad to think back that my parents had to die never having the chance to be reunited. Uncle Heinrich died of starvation in Siberia. My dad died in a country of the free... Canada.

For us in Canada, we can visit our loved ones at their gravesites. But for the ones that were buried out in the woods, they are lost forever. I feel sorry for the three survivors left from Uncle Heinrich's family that has no gravesite to visit. Just the memories are left in our hearts. I am so thankful that my family, were one of the lucky ones. My father and mother didn't end up in Siberia; we stayed together as a family. And my parents were able to have their remaining years living in a peaceful country.

I was eager to bring out the information that I had gathered in my second book. I wanted to document the occurrences that happened during the war and after to some of my siblings who were too young to remember the brutality that the German people endured. The rich landlords had the upper hand over the poor; people who were kept in slavery. The motto was, "Do as I say, or you'll be out on the street".

After revealing all of this information. My sister-in-law Margaret let me in on a secret that she had been carrying for years.

Margaret began revealing her secret.

> "While you are bringing up all of these things about your own mother and Grandma's life. I'm going to tell you about my own mother.
>
> After my mother passed away, my stepfather Edward Ebinger told me of the secret that my mother was keeping from her children. My mother Ida was working for a rich landowner. The young landowner had fathered two little girls with my mother. She was hoping one day to

get married. My mother was a poor girl with no inheritance to bring.

When the girls reached the age of about four or five years old, the girls were taken away from my mother. My mother was chased off the land and told to move far away and never to come back if she likes to stay alive.

Still today, I have two sisters somewhere in the world probably never ever to meet".

My mother was so secretive. She never talked about her past. When I asked her, she simply replied, "I don't know" or "I don't remember". All I know, my mother died of a broken heart.

So many things were kept a secret. It was feared that it would be taken as if the mother was a bad girl. Most times this was not the case, it was, "do as I say or you'll be out on the street". Some people took the hurt so badly that they couldn't bear to relive the past, and they took the heartache to their graves. Margaret said, "and that was my mom".

After reading the book "Khrushchev Remembers" by Edward Crankshaw, I wanted to share the horrors from his book.

"The Stalingrad's Front"

"Yeremenko" was the commander of the Stalingrad front. Yeremenko and his army encircled the Paulus Army in the fall and finished it off in the winter. Khrushchev remembered seeing a horrible scene moving into the city of Stalingrad. The troops were busy gathering the corpses of German soldiers. With spring approaching, and a hot summer ahead it was necessary to dispose of the bodies before decomposition started and an epidemic would break out. The ground was still frozen and was difficult to dig out the bodies from the frozen ground. Thousands of corpses were stacked in layers, alternating layers of bodies' then railway ties. Gasoline was poured over the pile of dead bodies and set on fire. Khrushchev went to the area to watch, but left and never went back to the site again. The horrible scene of burning bodies, and the retched smell was overwhelming.

Around Stalingrad many German soldiers were laying on the ground stripped of their clothing from their waist down; their trousers and boots missing. It was the work of the pillagers. Khrushchev was sorry to say that it was the doing of civilians and soldiers doing the pillaging.

As they pushed forward after the battle of Stalingrad, they saw the dead bodies of soldiers stacked in piles. Khrushchev had asked General Volski if these men were shot. He replied that they were all killed in battle. Khrushchev didn't rule out the possibility that some of his men had violated our strict instructions not to use force against the prisoners. It wasn't wanted to give the enemy any propaganda that we were shooting the captives. However it was understandable that some of our soldiers may have taken their revenge out on their own. They were killing any fascist enemy soldier that they could in the occupied Soviet territory.

Looking Back

It could have been possible that some of my own people could have been the ones being victims. There still today many people who have never been found and are listed as M. I. A.

This little poem is in memory of our forefathers and all of our loved ones who have perished...suffering from starvation, hunger, torture and murder in Siberia under the communist regime and WW11.

Anna Fischer

Dear Ancestors

Your tombstone stands among the rest
Neglected and alone
The names and date are chiseled out
On polished marble stone
It reaches out to all who care
It is not too late to mourn
You did not know that I exist
You died, and then I was born
Yet each of us are cells of you
In flesh, in blood, in bone
Our blood contracts and beats a pulse
Entirely not our own
Dear Ancestors the place you filled
Many years ago
Spreads out among the ones you left
Who would have love you so
I wonder if you lived and loved
I wonder if you know
That someday I will find this spot
And come to visit you
Then we will walk hand in hand
Waiting for someone to find
Our lonely spot too.

Author Unknown